DECIDE
TO
THRIVE

**SIX CHOICES FOR LIFE CHANGE
THAT *REALLY* WORK**

STEVE ROBINSON

DECIDE TO THRIVE: SIX CHOICES FOR LIFE CHANGE THAT *REALLY* WORK

DEDICATION

For my wife, Jennifer, my confidante, my friend, my love.

*For my children, who continue to inspire me
and make me proud.*

*For the team at Church of the King, whose commitment
and dedication to reaching people and building lives
is impacting people around the world.*

TABLE OF CONTENTS

CHAPTER 1

SIX DECISIONS THAT WILL CHANGE YOUR LIFE

In this book, we answer two big questions: One, *What does a thriving life really look like?* And two, *How can we get—and stay—there?*

No matter who you are, how old you are, or where you're from, these two questions are relevant to your life. Maybe you can relate to where I once was–searching for a relationship with God, wondering what He's like, and searching for how to live differently. Perhaps that's where you are, wondering who God is, what is He like, and whether or not He actually cares about you. Or maybe you participate in religious duties. You try to live a good life, but deep down, you feel like something's missing.

Deep down, you know you were meant for more, but you're not sure what that "more" is or how to find it. If that's you, I have very good news. God has *the* answers to our deepest questions. There is a pathway that leads to a life filled with peace, purpose, and significance. Your life can look like a thriving forest, bursting with vibrancy, regardless of your circumstances.

Within these pages, I talk about six daily decisions, rooted in six biblical values, that result in a thriving life.

It all starts with the unique ability God has given to humanity: *the power to decide.*

THE POWER TO DECIDE

In the 1930s, the Great Depression and the Dust Bowl forced thousands of families to leave their homes in search of a better life. One individual was Florence Owens Thompson, a widowed mother of seven children.[1]

After losing work due to the plummeting economy and severe dust storms in Oklahoma, Florence made the difficult decision to migrate to California. At thirty-two, she left home with her seven children to find work and provide for her family, despite the overwhelming adversity.

---

[1] Dorothea Lange, *Destitute Pea Pickers in California. Mother of Seven Children. Age Thirty-two. Nipomo, California*, 1936, photograph, Library of Congress, Accessed October 17, 2024, https://www.loc.gov/pictures/item/2017762891/.

Destitute pea pickers in California. Mother of seven children. Age thirty-two. Nipomo, California. Photograph taken by Dorothea Lange in 1936.

In 1936, while camped by the roadside after their car broke down, Florence was photographed by Dorothea Lange, creating the iconic image known as "Migrant Mother." This photograph became a symbol of resilience against the struggles faced by many during that era.[2] Florence's decision helped her transcend from a victim of circumstance to a woman building a better life for herself and her children. And hers wasn't an isolated incident.

According to historical records, during the 1930s, approximately 2.5 million people fled the Dust Bowl states, with about two hundred thousand moving to California. This mass migration was one of the largest in American history, highlighting how pivotal decisions reshaped countless lives during that period.[3]

You are where you are today because of the decisions you've made.

You are where you are today because of the decisions you've made. Other people's decisions may influence us, but they don't define us. Regardless of your upbringing or circumstances, you have the power to decide to move beyond them and thrive in life.

We find the reason in the very beginning. In Genesis 1:26–28, we read:

---

[2] Don Nardo, *Migrant Mother: How a Photograph Defined the Great Depression.* (Compass Point Books, 2011), 6–9.

[3] James N. Gregory, *American Exodus: The Dust Bowl Migration and Okie Culture in California.* (New York: Oxford University Press, 1991).

Then God said, "Let Us make man in Our image, according to Our likeness; let them have dominion over the fish of the sea, over the birds of the air, and over the cattle, over all the earth and over every creeping thing that creeps on the earth." So God created man in His *own* image; in the image of God He created him; male and female He created them. Then God blessed them, and God said to them, "Be fruitful and multiply; fill the earth and subdue it; have dominion over the fish of the sea, over the birds of the air, and over every living thing that moves on the earth."

This passage reveals something profound about our nature. We are created in the image of God; the Latin term is *imago Dei*. This means we have been endowed by our Creator with the capacity to think, reason, and make choices that shape our lives and impact the world around us.

Unlike the animal kingdom, where decisions are based on instinct, appetite, risk, and survival, we have the capability to create environments where people can flourish, both for ourselves and others. The Bible says we're not only made in the image of God, but we've also been given dominion. Scripture is clear: we're not just created to survive, we're called to thrive and to help others do the same.[4]

What would the world look like if everyone understood this about themselves, and better yet, met the God who made them? Friend, my prayer is that by reading this book, you will meet the God who loves you and created you.

---

[4] Proverbs 11:28. "… the righteous will thrive like a green leaf" (NIV).

You have the power to make decisions and move forward, regardless of what adversity may come your way. We all do. This means no one should remain a victim of circumstance. Instead, we have the opportunity to rise above our circumstances to become a product of our decisions.

Victimhood is the most disempowering state in which we can exist. Although circumstances may have been unjust and painful, you still have the power to move beyond their impact and thrive in life.

Making a conscious decision to have a better life isn't enough. Our decisions to thrive need to align with three criteria:

GOD'S WORD

GOD'S WILL

GOD'S WAY

Most of us have seen a movie with a superhero who can fly. Picture a little boy wearing a cape who decides with all his might that he can fly. Yet the moment he jumps from his bed, gravity gets the final say and a trip to the ER is in store. That's how gravity works.

In a similar fashion, our ignorance and stubbornness can cause us to resist God's Word, which unfortunately results in a life filled with pain. Life is hard enough on its own, but resisting God makes it tougher.

Now, wouldn't it be nice to cooperate with God, knowing your decisions align with His Will? Think about it. How different would your life look if you made decisions that you knew without the shadow of a doubt would create a thriving life? Decisions simple enough to make every day, yet powerful enough to change everything for the better?

When we align our lives with God's purposes, everything changes for the better.

I wrote this book to share just that: six decisions that make it possible for you to build a thriving life. You can *decide* to thrive. Before we do a flyover summary of the decisions, it's worth asking, *What does thriving actually mean?*

WHAT DOES IT MEAN TO THRIVE?

Over the past three decades, I've had the privilege to walk alongside thousands in their journey of discovering God's best for their lives. Here's what I've learned: when we align our lives with God's purposes, everything changes for the better.

But do you know what really motivates and challenges me? It's those people who've been hit with every challenge you can think of, yet they are filled with joy and thrive despite adversity. These are the ones whose challenges have actually deepened their faith rather than erased it.

A number of years ago, a couple in our church tragically lost a child. That is one of the most soul-crushing pains people can endure. However, what they did with their pain is remarkable. They began to help other families. Even today, they are thriving and continue to impact others with hope and encouragement. It's amazing how God can transform our pain into a platform to help others.

Their story reminds me of what my friend and bestselling author, Jon Gordon, says. "Everyone will experience adversity and change, but how you respond is what matters most."[5]

In John 16:33, Jesus Himself said we'd have challenges in life.[6] However, His half-brother James described how the thriving Christian can respond to challenges in James 1:2–4:

My brethren, count it all joy when you fall into various trials, knowing that the testing of your faith produces patience. But let

---

[5] Jon Gordon (@Jongordon11), "Everyone will experience adversity and change. How you respond is what matters most," Twitter (now X), April 6, 2019, https://x.com/JonGordon11/status/1114501434580656128.

[6] John 16:33. "These things I have spoken to you, that in Me you may have peace. In the world you will have tribulation; but be of good cheer, I have overcome the world."

patience have *its* perfect work, that you may be perfect and complete, lacking nothing.

At this point, you might be wondering what kind of a book on thriving you picked up! But as you'll learn, adversity can serve to strengthen us. Thriving is also more than succeeding in one area of our lives. To thrive means we flourish and move forward in every area of our lives.

When we do things God's way, here's what our lives can look like:

- **Spiritually:** Becoming dynamically connected to God in a growing relationship.

- **Mentally:** Having clarity of mind and peace in your thoughts.

- **Emotionally:** Coming to a place where you can experience a wide range of emotions without them hijacking your day.

- **Physically:** Living with strength to fulfill your purpose.

- **Financially:** Having your needs met and being in a position to be generous to help others.

- **Relationally:** Building deep, meaningful connections.

- **Vocationally:** Finding purpose and fulfillment in your work.

That sounds like the kind of life we all want. No matter the challenges we face, people who build their lives upon God's Word, Will, and Way don't allow challenging circumstances to dominate their lives.

A clear picture of a thriving life is found in Jeremiah 17:7–8:

Blessed *is* the man who trusts in the Lord, and whose hope is the Lord. For he shall be like a tree planted by the waters, which spreads out its roots by the river, and will not fear when heat comes; but its leaf will be green, and will not be anxious in the year of drought, nor will cease from yielding fruit.

Talk about a thriving life!

All the "drought" *out there* can't stop the flowing water. The desert heat and the pains of life can't wither the tree's vibrant leaves. Its branches are full of abundant fruit.

This is what you can expect from a thriving life. Sounds wonderful, doesn't it?

That reminds me of a tough season, a number of years where we were all impacted by COVID. I noticed the people who stayed connected to God and maintained life-giving relationships continued to thrive in that difficult time.

A tree that thrives doesn't just exist, it bears fruit. The next question is, how do we bear fruit for more than a single season? A fruit tree that only produces once is living below its full potential.

There are plenty of great books about "doing," and many others about "being." I want to help you do both in this book. To produce the kind of fruitful life Scripture promises means making decisions rooted in six biblical values. (You'll learn each value alongside the corresponding daily decision in the chapters ahead.)

Here's the biblical template for life change that really works:

6 DAILY DECISIONS	VALUES ROOTED IN	CREATE A THRIVING LIFE IN EVERY AREA
> THE PRIORITY DECISION > THE RELATIONSHIP DECISION > THE PURPOSE DECISION > THE GROWTH DECISION > THE INFLUENCE DECISION > THE GENEROSITY DECISION	> GOD'S WORD > GOD'S WILL > GOD'S WAY	> SPIRITUALLY > MENTALLY > EMOTIONALLY > PHYSICALLY > FINANCIALLY > RELATIONALLY > VOCATIONALLY

BUILT TO LAST

Even the business world knows that good things that last and have an enduring impact are built well. In his landmark book, *Built to Last*, author Jim Collins studied companies that endured for generations. What sets them apart? Why did they survive— *and even thrive*—when many others failed?

Collins shares several key characteristics, but here's what I've found most helpful. He said enduring companies stay true to their core values and purpose.[7] Even though stocks fluctuate and technology changes faster than a bullet train, some things remain

---

[7] Jerry I. Porras and James C. Collins. *Built to Last: Successful Habits of Visionary Companies*. (Harper Business, 1994).

the same. Certain principles and values are worth building your company–and in our case, your life–upon.

I think it's helpful to look at businesses because they are a collection of people joined for a common purpose. As followers of Jesus, we function similarly. We all thrive together as each of us builds upon the biblical values rooted in God's Word, Will, and Way! This is how *thriving* lasts for a lifetime—rather than a season.

In Matthew 7, Jesus gives us the ultimate blueprint for building a life that can withstand challenges, overcome adversity, and thrive continually. In verses 24–27, He says:

> "Therefore whoever hears these sayings of Mine, and does them, I will liken him to a wise man who built his house on the rock: and the rain descended, the floods came, and the winds blew and beat on that house; and it did not fall, for it was founded on the rock. But everyone who hears these sayings of Mine, and does not do them, will be like a foolish man who built his house on the sand: and the rain descended, the floods came, and the winds blew and beat on that house; and it fell. And great was its fall."

Jesus is saying that rain is going to fall on all of us. Floods of adversity will hit you. Life is going to batter you. But a strong foundation keeps you from falling apart. This is the question Jesus is posing here: *What are you building your life upon?*

So, let me ask, are you properly prepared for the storms of life? In a day and time when things are rapidly shifting around us, the way to prepare is to build your life upon the enduring values found in God's Word.

THE SIX DAILY DECISIONS

Strong foundations are built upon daily decisions to live out biblical values. This book is divided into six daily decisions based upon six biblical values. Each decision stands on its own but is intricately connected to the others. Together, and over time, they'll create a thriving ecosystem of habits, mindsets, beliefs, behaviors, character, and results.

> *Strong foundations are built upon daily decisions to live out biblical values.*

Remember, you can read and apply this book on your own, with a small group, or even as a church. The main thing is this: it's important to follow through on each decision. You will get out of this guide what you put into it.

The Priority Decision: I choose to put God first.

Discovering the joy of following Jesus daily.

The Relationship Decision: I choose to pursue life-giving relationships.

Connecting with others for life change.

The Purpose Decision: I choose to reach people for Christ.

Making an eternal impact by sharing my faith with others.

The Growth Decision: I choose to grow daily and help others do the same.

Embracing a lifetime of personal discipleship and making disciples.

The Influence Decision: I choose to make a difference through my unique gifts, talents, and abilities.

Serving others to help them thrive.

The Generosity Decision: I choose to live generously.

Experiencing the freedom of living open-handed.

Practiced together, the results from these six powerful decisions will compound. Just one apple seed can produce a tree. The next tree can produce more apples and more seeds. Until, in a small amount of time, you have innumerable orchards.

DECIDE TO ALIGN WITH GOD'S VALUES

Have you ever heard the story of Joseph from the book of Genesis? It's one of the most inspirational examples of how our decisions position and empower you to live a thriving life. Regardless of the pain and adversity we face in life, you are where you are today because of the decisions you make.

Joseph's story is the perfect illustration—it begins with betrayal.

Joseph's brothers had it out for him. You see, he was their father's favorite son. This so enraged his brothers that they threw him in a pit, wanting to kill him. At the last minute, they sold him to slave traders, returning to their father with a lie that a wild animal killed him.

From that pit of betrayal, Joseph had a Growth Decision to make—would he become bitter or better?

He ended up in Egypt, serving in the house of a wealthy man named Potiphar. As we see in Genesis 39:4, "Joseph found favor in his eyes and became his attendant" (New International Version). He worked hard. He was the best worker anyone could hope for.

Things seemed to be going well—until Potiphar's wife set out to seduce him.

Joseph did more than spurn her advance. He couldn't even conceive of making a decision out of alignment with his values. In Genesis 39:9 he said: "How then could I do such a wicked thing and sin against God" (NIV)? His decision to honor God led to false accusations. In turn, our exemplary man, Joseph, was thrown into prison. Not for a night—but for thirteen years.

In prison, Joseph again could have become bitter. Instead, he made another pivotal decision: to use his God-given gifts to serve others. He interpreted dreams for his fellow prisoners. Yet it wasn't until years later this decision bore fruit.

As God had planned, Pharaoh began to have troubling dreams. Through a miraculous set of events, Joseph was summoned from the prison to the palace to interpret those dreams, even when others had failed.

Here was Joseph's response: "I cannot do it, but God will give Pharaoh the answer he desires."[8] In miraculous fashion, he interprets Pharaoh's dreams and rises to second-in-command. Joseph thrived through every circumstance because of his decisions. Joseph *decided* to thrive. From the bottom of a pit to a wretched prison, Joseph's decisions aligned with God's Word, Will, and Way.

In years to follow, while serving as Pharaoh's right-hand man, Joseph made the Influence Decision that saved countless lives during a severe famine. Not only Egyptians, but also his own family.

And what were Joseph's words to his brothers after reuniting? In Genesis 50:20 he said: "You intended to harm me, but God intended it for good to accomplish what is now being done,

---

[8] Genesis 41:16 (NIV).

the saving of many lives" (NIV). What an example of putting God's Word, Will, and Way first! At each critical turn—the pit, Potiphar's house, the prison, and the palace—Joseph's decisions laid the groundwork for a thriving life in spite of adversity.

Here are the decisions he made to lay that groundwork:

- He made the Priority Decision every time he put God first over his own comfort and convenience.

- He made the Relationship Decision when he kept helping his prison mates and forgave his brothers for what they'd done to him.

- He made the Growth Decision every time he chose to be *better* instead of growing *bitter*.

- He made the Influence Decision by serving countless others through the great famine.

The same principles hold true for us today. When we make decisions aligned with God's *Word*, *Will*, and *Way*, He positions us to fulfill His divine purpose. A thriving life is based on our partnership with God and our obedience to Him.

You are only six decisions away from a thriving life. If you're ready to start, turn the page. It's time to talk about the first decision you need to make as you wake up every day.

CHAPTER 2

DECISION 1:
THE PRIORITY DECISION

I CHOOSE TO PUT GOD FIRST

The very thing holding us back, at times, is the life we think we want. However, that "ideal life" can turn out much less than advertised.

One night, as a college freshman, I learned this truth firsthand. I was studying alone and put my head in my hands, wondering how on earth I ended up so lost and empty. The things that were supposed to make me happy kept losing their luster. You go to college, meet new people, hang out, and study a little bit so you can hopefully get a good job one day.

At first, that had worked. I had nonstop fun hopping from party to party. Friends came fast and easy. I partied through my first three months. This is what the movies show a thriving collegiate life looks like—right? However, a gnawing emptiness caught up with me. I found myself asking, is this all there is?

If you're wondering the same, I want you to know two things: One, you're not alone. And two, there are answers. Uncovering these answers is the most important journey you'll ever embark on. In fact, it's more important than choosing a career, finding a spouse, or achieving your dreams.

In this chapter, we'll define the first decision for building a thriving life: **The Priority Decision**. You must decide to put God first every day. Why? Things get out of whack quickly when you don't recognize God's involvement in your life.

WHERE'S YOUR LADDER LEANING?

Thomas Merton said, "People may spend their whole lives climbing the ladder of success only to find, once they reach the top, that the ladder is leaning against the wrong wall."[9]

My friend, have you paused long enough to look up at the wall your ladder of life leans against? Do you see the top? Is it actually where you want to go?

The truth is, if your priorities are out of whack, your ladder is leaned against the wrong wall.

You see, your priorities in life determine the wall you're climbing. As we saw in the last chapter, a thriving life is aligned with God's Word, Will, and Way. A thriving life leans against the

---

[9] Stephen R. Covey, *The 7 Habits of Highly Effective People: Restoring the Character Ethic.* (Rosetta Books, 2021).

wall that matters for eternity. Work, goals, and success have their place. Yet we must be careful how we allow them to define and direct us. You see, whatever or whoever has our hope also has our heart. In Matthew 6:21, Jesus put it this way, "For where your treasure is, there your heart will be also."

Whatever or whoever has our hope also has our heart.

Your first priority is found where you place your ultimate hope for a thriving life. The great thing is you have a moment right now to stop climbing, look up, and decide which wall your ladder will lean against.

THE CHALLENGE OF PUTTING GOD FIRST

Before we dive into how to put God first, we need to address why it's so challenging in the first place. The root of this challenge goes all the way back to the beginning—to Genesis 3.

In the Garden of Eden, Adam and Eve enjoyed a perfect relationship with God. But then Satan, the ultimate antagonist, entered the scene. One of the profound lies he tempted them with can be paraphrased this way: "God is withholding something good from you."[10] This deception led to the first sin

---

[10] "Now the serpent was more cunning than any beast of the field which the LORD God had made. And he said to the woman, "Has God indeed said, 'You shall not eat of every tree of the garden'?"

and, suddenly, the clear connection between God and humanity was severed.

This event, known as the Fall, had far-reaching consequences. From that point on, every human being has been born with a sinful nature. This innate tendency to live life on our own terms is the primary obstacle to putting Him first.

Unfortunately, it's not just our internal struggle with sin that makes prioritizing God difficult. We also face an external enemy. In 2 Corinthians 4:4, the apostle Paul tells us:

Satan, who is the god of this world, has blinded the minds of those who don't believe. They are unable to see the glorious light of the Good News. They don't understand this message about the glory of Christ, who is the exact likeness of God (New Living Translation).

So we're dealing with a double challenge: the sin within us and Satan's influence from without. Both of these factors left unchecked can skew our decision-making abilities. We end up building our lives with our ladder leaning on the wrong wall.

THE BEDROCK TRUTH

Back to my story. As a college freshman I realized my ladder was certainly leaning against the wrong wall. I was at a profound crossroads in my life. Shortly after the night when I found my head in my hands with more questions than answers, I was invited to a college Bible study. Divine timing was at work. My heart was ready for something different. Something I could build my life upon that brought fulfillment and peace. I reluctantly went to the Bible study on October 28, 1987, and met Christ in a way that radically changed the trajectory of my life. I repented of my sin and surrendered my life to Jesus. He saved my life!

From that moment on, I knew my biggest priority had shifted. In my new relationship with Jesus, I found fulfillment, peace, and a new purpose.

Here's the bedrock truth that changed everything for me, and I believe it can change everything for you too: *You were created by God, for God, to live out God's purpose for your life.*

Let that sink in for a moment…

You're not an accident.

You're not a cosmic coincidence.

You're not slime plus time.

In Ephesians 2:10, God calls you the *work of His hands.*[11] This means He created you for a reason.

That reason, first and foremost, is to know Him. Not just to know about Him, but to truly know Him in a deep, personal way.

---

[11] Ephesians 2:10. "For we are God's handiwork, created in Christ Jesus to do good works, which God prepared in advance for us to do" (NIV).

Once you have surrendered to Christ and have a personal relationship with Him, it's important to keep Him as the first priority daily. Don't forget about your relationship with God. He wants to be involved in your everyday life. Now—keep Him as your top priority. Everything else in life—your career, your relationships, your achievements—all flow from your primary relationship with God.

When you make the daily decision to put God first, everything else begins to make sense–one decision at a time. You'll realize things like prayer are far more important than just a once-a-morning ritual. It's about connecting with God and talking with Him throughout your day.

Imagine what your business meetings would look like if you uttered a quiet prayer for wisdom before walking in. Picture asking God for an open heart when it's time to have a difficult talk with your teenager. Think about the benefit of talking to God–who knows everything–when considering moving to a new city. This is how you live out the Priority Decision. Who do you look to for guidance? What values guide your decisions?

Putting God first really comes to life when we live this way. Here's how you put God first: When you face any situation, you ask the question, "What does God's Word say about this?" This is why I encourage people to develop a daily habit of Bible reading and prayer.

Having these constant conversations with God and looking to His Word are where you really get to *know* who God is and what His will is. When we talk about knowing God, I want to be clear—we're not simply talking knowing facts *about* God. It's about a personal, intimate relationship *with* God.

It's a lot like collecting sports cards as a kid. There's a big difference between knowing a professional athlete's stats on the back of their card and actually knowing the person. This isn't about religious rituals or just following a set of rules. It's about connecting with the living God through the person of Jesus Christ.

You see, God isn't some distant, impersonal force. He's not an angry judge waiting for you to mess up. He's a loving Father who wants connection with His kids. When we prioritize that connection, we change and so does our entire outlook on life.

C. S. Lewis, the renowned author who journeyed from atheism to faith, put it this way, "I believe in Christianity as I believe that the sun has risen: not only because I see it, but because by it I see everything else."[12] When we come to know God, everything else in life comes into focus.

There's a man in Scripture named Nicodemus who learned this firsthand. He was a very important leader in his day. Nicodemus was the man who seemingly had it all together. But something

---

[12] C.S. Lewis: "Is Theology Poetry?" in *The Weight of Glory* (HarperOne, 2001).

was missing, and he knew it. John 3:1–21 recounts Nicodemus going to see Jesus one night. He was looking for answers.

He came to Jesus under the cover of darkness, perhaps afraid of what others might think. During this encounter, Jesus told him something that challenged him: "You must be born again."[13] Nicodemus scratched his head, and to paraphrase, said, "But how can my mother give birth to me again? That just doesn't make sense!"

But Jesus, as usual, had something much deeper in mind. He didn't mean physically. He meant spiritually. All of Nicodemus's religious knowledge and good deeds weren't enough. He needed a complete spiritual rebirth, a new life with God at the center.

Like Nicodemus, many people today are realizing success, knowledge, and religious activity aren't enough. They need a personal relationship with God. Maybe that's you. Perhaps you've achieved everything you thought would make you happy, yet you're still feeling empty inside. Or maybe you've been religious all your life, but you've never experienced an intimate, personal relationship with God.

Here's the amazing thing: God's love for you isn't based on your performance. You don't have to clean yourself up first or reach a certain level of goodness. God loves you right where you are, and He's inviting you into a relationship with Him.

---

[13] John 3:7. "Do not marvel that I said to you, 'You must be born again'."

The apostle Paul puts it this way in Romans 5:8: "But God demonstrates His own love toward us, in that while we were still sinners, Christ died for us." God didn't wait for us to get our act together. He made the first move. He reached out to us when we were at our worst.

YOUR MOST IMPORTANT DECISION

In Matthew 16:13–20, Jesus asks *the most important question* to the disciples. They're traveling into a region called Caesarea Philippi. They discuss what others were saying about Jesus's identity. Then, the moment arrives in verses 15–17.

Jesus asks, "But who do you say that I am?"

Peter answers, "You are the Christ, the Son of the living God."

Jesus replies, "Blessed are you, Simon Bar-Jonah, for flesh and blood has not revealed this to you, but My Father who is in Heaven. And I also say to you that you are Peter, and on this rock I will build My church."

At that moment, Jesus wanted to know what His disciples believed. Because ultimately, your relationship with God starts with Who you believe Jesus is. And it was Peter's revelation of Who Jesus is that became the rock Christ would build His church upon!

Friend, Jesus is asking you the same question right now: "Who do you say that I am?" What you decide about Jesus is the most important choice you will ever make. Period. Everything else flows from it. There is simply no thriving in life without Christ at the center.

You might be wondering, "Can't I just go to church and be a good person? Isn't that basically what God wants me to do?"

The trouble is, neither you nor I could ever be *good enough* in our own power. The Bible puts it like this in Romans 3:23: "For all have sinned and fall short of the glory of God." This falling short is called sin. Romans 6:23 shows us both the gravity of our problem and the gift God offers: "For the wages of sin is death, but the gift of God is eternal life in Christ Jesus our Lord."

Right now, the most wonderful gift in the universe is waiting for you: eternal life in Christ! Whether you're ready to put your faith in Christ for the first time—or recommit your life to Him—Now is your time. Romans 10:9–10 tells us:

that if you confess with your mouth the Lord Jesus and believe in your heart that God has raised Him from the dead, you will be saved. For with the heart one believes unto righteousness, and with the mouth confession is made unto salvation.

Confess that Jesus is Lord.

Believe He died in your place on the cross and was raised from the dead.

You will be saved!

Now, if you're ready to make the decision to follow Christ, pray this prayer with me out loud and you will be saved!

Heavenly Father, I recognize that You created me for a relationship with You. Today, I choose to put You first in my life. I confess that Jesus is both my Savior and Lord. That He died in my place to save me from my sin and to give me eternal life. I commit to seeking You daily and following Your ways. From this moment forward, help me to prioritize my relationship with You in every area of my life. Thank You for Your love, grace, and salvation. In Jesus's name. Amen.

Praise God! If you prayed that prayer and believed it in your heart you are saved and now God's child. Your adventure is just beginning. Your decision about who Jesus is sets you up for making the Priority Decision every day. There will be challenges and moments of uncertainty, yet as you consistently choose to put God first, you'll discover a life of purpose, peace, and joy you never thought possible.

YOUR DAILY DECISION TO PUT GOD FIRST

After I came to Christ, I was fortunate to get plugged into a great church and be surrounded by godly men who discipled me. One of the things I learned early on was that my decision to give my life to Jesus was just the beginning. I also realized my daily decision to follow His Word, Will, and Way was of primary importance.

Even in the face of death, Jesus submitted His life to the Father, saying, "Nevertheless, not My will but Yours be done."[14] *That* is our model of the Priority Decision in action. Of the staggering thirty-five thousand decisions we make each day, the decisions to put God's will first shape our life most.[15]

Let me be clear with you, friend. Just because I'm a pastor doesn't mean I don't struggle with this too. As human beings living in a fallen world, making the daily recommitment to God's priorities over our own isn't a walk in the park.

Over the years, I've found six big obstacles that get in our way. Are they real? Yes. But are they insurmountable? Not at all!

Let's take them one by one.

1. Busyness

We make time for what we value. If you're too busy to deepen your relationship with your Creator, check if your ladder is leaning against the wrong wall. Begin small. Set aside just five minutes a day to pray and read your

---

[14] Luke 22:42. "Father, if it is Your will, take this cup away from Me; nevertheless not My will, but Yours, be done."

[15] Joel Hoomans, "35,000 Decisions: The Great Choices of Strategic Leaders," The Leading Edge (blog), Roberts Wesleyan University, March 20, 2015, https://go.roberts.edu/leadingedge/the-great-choices-of-strategic-leaders.

Bible. You'll be amazed at how God will multiply that time. Soon, five minutes turns into longer periods you simply cannot live without.

2. Past hurts

I'm truly sorry if you've been hurt, abused, or taken advantage of in life. However, please don't let those hurts keep you from experiencing the love of God. He's not like those who hurt you. He is perfect. Mankind is not. Give Him the opportunity to show you who He really is. The issue with past hurts is they can become your focus rather than God. If you're always looking backward to the past, it's hard to look up to God and forward to your future. You are not powerless. You can make the decision to move beyond victimhood into a thriving relationship with God.

3. Doubt

Doubt isn't the opposite of faith; it's part of faith. God is big enough to handle your doubts. Bring them to Him. Wrestle with them. Some of the most well-known believers in history have gone through periods of doubt. The key is to keep seeking, keep asking questions. If you're wrestling with doubt, don't let it knock you out of the ring. Instead, follow Jesus's instruction in Matthew 7:7: "Ask, and it will be given to you; seek, and you will find; knock, and it will be opened to you."

4. Fear of Missing Out (FOMO)

Let's be honest, FOMO is real! You might worry that putting God first means giving up on fun or success. Remember Satan whispering lies to Eve? He wanted her focused on what she thought she didn't have, rather than on the beautiful garden she got to live in! Is FOMO clouding your ability to see everything God has already given you? If you struggle with FOMO, make the choice to live gratefully and to tell God *thank you* for something different each day. Keep your eyes looking up.

5. Worry about what others will think

It can be scary to go against the tide of culture. But remember, you weren't created to fit in—you were created to stand out for God. Your boldness might even inspire others to consider their own relationship with God.

6. Uncertainty about God's plans

Trusting God with your life can feel risky—especially if it's new. But His plans for you are better than anything you could dream up for yourself. As it says in Jeremiah 29:11: "'For I know the plans I have for you,' declares the Lord, 'plans to prosper you and not to harm you, plans to give you hope and a future'" (NIV). God gave this promise to the Israelites when they were in exile in Babylon. What this tells me is that even if you're in a tough situation right now, facing extreme adversity, God still has a good plan for you. Trust Him, put Him first, and watch what happens.

Remember, putting God first isn't about being perfect. It's about setting your heart's direction and committing to follow God one step at a time.

HOW TO PUT GOD FIRST

So, how do you actually implement the Priority Decision in your daily life? Here are some practical steps:

1. **Start your day with God:** I set aside time each morning for prayer and Bible reading. Romans 12:1 instructs us to "…present your bodies a living sacrifice, holy, acceptable to God, which is your reasonable service." Prioritizing time with Him is submitting ourselves to Christ! If you're just starting out, you can find lots of great Bible reading plans on the YouVersion Bible App.

2. **Seek God's guidance in decision making:** Before making decisions, big or small, ask for God's wisdom. James 1:5 promises, "If any of you lacks wisdom, let him ask of God, who gives to all liberally and without reproach, and it will be given to him." You can expect to hear His voice in three primary ways. One, through the Bible. Two, the inner witness of the Holy Spirit. Three, through godly counsel with other believers. Over time, you will recognize God's voice better and clearer.[16]

---

[16] John 10:27. "My sheep hear My voice, and I know them, and they follow me."

3. **Prioritize church and small group involvement:** Surround yourself with a community that encourages your faith. Hebrews 10:24–25 reminds us that spending quality time with fellow believers isn't an extracurricular activity—it's paramount to our spiritual formation.

4. **Use your gifts to serve others:** Look for ways to bless others and advance God's Kingdom. 1 Peter 4:10 says, "As each one has received a gift, minister it to one another, as good stewards of the manifold grace of God."

5. **Steward your resources for God's glory:** Manage your time, talents, and treasure with eternity in mind (more on this in the Generosity Decision). Again, Jesus told us in Matthew 6:21, "For where your treasure is, there your heart will be also." The truth is, where you spend your money, time, and energy shows your greatest priorities.

Remember, these are not about earning God's love, but about growing in your relationship with Him and allowing Him to work through you on a daily basis.

Reflect

Take some time to process these questions, either in personal reflection or with others in your small group. Growth happens best in community, but honest individual reflection is essential for lasting change.

To finish, I want to leave you with some questions to reflect on:

1. What are you hoping to gain or learn from this book?

2. How would you describe your current relationship with God? Is it close and personal, distant and formal, or somewhere in between?

3. What's one area where you'd like to grow in knowing God better? Maybe it's in prayer, or in understanding His Word, or in experiencing His presence in your daily life?

4. What are the challenges preventing you from prioritizing God in every area of your life?

5. How does knowing God's unconditional love, shown by sending His Son to die for you, influence your decision to put Him first?

6. What's one step you can take this week to pursue a deeper relationship with God?

Take some time to think about these questions. Write down your answers to reflect upon. Remember, this is a journey. You don't have to have it all figured out right away.

Act

Here's your action step: Start a daily habit of connecting with God.

Set aside some time each day for prayer and Bible reading. I pray through the *Lord's Prayer* each day in a topical fashion. For more information and access to resources to grow your prayer life, visit SteveRobinson.com/pray. If you're not sure where to start, begin with the Gospel of John. And write down any insights or questions you have in the simple S.O.A.P. format:

S—Scripture: What Scripture are you reading?

O—Observation: What do you think God's saying?

A—Application: How does it apply to your life?

P—Prayer: What questions, requests, or gratitude do you have for God?

As you begin this journey of prioritizing God, I want to encourage you with these words from Jeremiah 29:13–14: "And you will seek Me and find *Me*, when you search for Me with all your heart. I will be found by you, says the Lord…" That's a promise for you too.

God isn't hiding from you. He wants to be found. He wants a relationship with you even more than you want one with Him. So seek Him. Pursue Him. The adventure of a lifetime awaits you.

Remember, you were created to know God. Everything else in life—your work, your relationships, your dreams—they all find their true meaning and purpose when they're rooted in this primary relationship.

In the next chapter, we're going to explore how this relationship with God leads to going deeper with others. But for now, focus on this truth—you are loved by God. He created you to know Him and make Him known.

Don't let another day go by without putting God first. Choosing to prioritize Him is deciding to thrive.

Pray

Lord, thank You for the gift of this day and the opportunity to put You first. Help me to recognize the areas where I've been building my life on the wrong foundation. Give me the courage to realign my priorities with Your will. As I step into this day, may my life reflect Your priorities and bring glory to Your name. In Jesus's name. Amen.

CHAPTER 3

DECISION 2:
THE RELATIONSHIP DECISION

I CHOOSE TO PURSUE
LIFE-GIVING RELATIONSHIPS

PICTURE A PORCUPINE. Not exactly the cuddliest creature, is it? With its thirty thousand quills, it seems designed for isolation rather than connection. When threatened, it has two responses: fight (by shooting out its quills) or flight (by running for the hills).

Sound familiar?

At times, we're not so different from porcupines. We all have our quirks, our defense mechanisms, our ways of keeping others at a distance. Maybe you've been hurt before, and now you're quick to put up your defenses at the first sign of potential pain. Or perhaps you tend to withdraw, convinced it's safer to be alone than risk being vulnerable.

We all get prickly sometimes, don't we? But here's the thing. While we may sometimes act like porcupines, we weren't created to live like them. God designed us for connection, for community, for relationships that encourage us, nurture us, help us grow, and at times…even challenge us.

This truth isn't just a nice spiritual idea—it's a scientific reality that's necessary for an individual to thrive.

In 2004, researchers at the National Scientific Council on the Developing Child made an interesting discovery. They learned that infants' brains actually are wired for connection from birth. Each relationship (positive or negative) has an effect on their intellectual, social, emotional, physical, behavioral, and moral development. When adults respond to an infant or toddler's needs, their brain creates neural pathways that will support healthy learning and development later in life.[17] This study highlighted what we instinctively know: human connection isn't just a luxury, it's a necessity for healthy development and thriving. Just as the young children in the study needed nurture to flourish, we, too, need meaningful relationships to become all that God designed us to be. Make the next decision for a thriving life: **The Relationship Decision.**

---

[17] National Scientific Council on the Developing Child, "Young Children Develop in an Environment of Relationships: Working Paper No. 1" (Center on the Developing Child at Harvard University, 2004), http://developingchild.harvard.edu/wp-content/uploads/2004/04/Young-Children-Develop-in-an-Environment-of-Relationships.pdf.

GOD'S DESIGN FOR CONNECTION

Let's go back to the beginning. In Genesis 2:18, we find a profound statement about our human nature—"And the Lord God said, 'It is not good that man should be alone…'" Now, this was before the Fall, before sin entered the world. Adam was in perfect communion with God, walking with Him in the cool of the day. Yet God looked at this man, made in His image, and declared that continual solitude was "not good."

This tells us something crucial about our design: we were made for a relationship not just with God, but with each other. We are, as the apostle Peter describes in 1 Peter 2:5, "…living stones…being built into a spiritual house" (NIV). Notice the imagery here—not isolated bricks laid end-to-end, but stones fitted together, supporting and complementing each other.

Think about it—a single stone, no matter how beautiful or well-formed, cannot make a house. It's only when stones are brought together, shaped to fit alongside one another, that they can create something greater than themselves. In the same way, we are meant to be part of something bigger than our individual lives. We are meant to be part of God's family.

This concept of community isn't just a New Testament idea. Throughout the Old Testament, we see God working through families, tribes, and nations. The Israelites were called to be a community that reflected God's character to the world. In the New Testament, this idea expands to the church—a global family united by faith in Christ.

In fact, the early Church provides us with a powerful example of how this kind of community can transform lives and impact the world. In Acts 2:42–47, we get a glimpse into their daily life:

> They devoted themselves to the apostles' teaching and to fellowship, to the breaking of bread and to prayer. Everyone was filled with awe at the many wonders and signs performed by the apostles. All the believers were together and had everything in common. They sold property and possessions to give to anyone who had need. Every day they continued to meet together in the temple courts. They broke bread in their homes and ate together with glad and sincere hearts, praising God and enjoying the favor of all the people. And the Lord added to their number daily those who were being saved (NIV).

This passage paints a picture of a community deeply connected not just in their beliefs, but also in their daily lives. They shared meals, resources, and time together. They supported each other practically and spiritually. The result? They experienced joy and saw miracles. The Church grew rapidly as others were drawn to the love and unity they witnessed.

The early Church shows us that when we truly live in community as God intended, it not only enriches our own lives but also becomes a powerful testimony to the world around us.

THE IMPACT OF RELATIONSHIPS ON WELL-BEING

As I mentioned earlier, research has consistently shown that people with strong social connections live longer, healthier lives than those who are isolated. One study found that the most isolated individuals were three times more likely to die prematurely than those with strong relational ties.[18] Remarkably, this held true even when comparing people with unhealthy habits and strong relationships with those with great health habits but weak social connections.

In other words, it really is better to eat a chocolate-glazed donut with good friends than to drink kale smoothies alone! (Maybe that's just my biased opinion…) But all jokes aside, why is this?

It's because God has placed within each of us what we might call a "human-shaped void." Just as there's a God-shaped void that only He can fill, there's also a space in our hearts that can only be filled by genuine human connection. We can try to fill it with success, with achievements, with possessions—but nothing quite fits like authentic relationships.

Mother Teresa, who dedicated her life to serving the poorest of the poor in Calcutta, India, once said that "Loneliness and

---

[18] Jessica Martino, Jennifer Pegg, and Elizabeth Pegg Frates, "The Connection Prescription: Using the Power of Social Interactions and the Deep Desire for Connectedness to Empower Health and Wellness," *American Journal of Lifestyle Medicine* 11, no. 6 (October 7, 2015): 466–475., doi:10.1177/1559827615608788.

the feeling of being unwanted is the most terrible poverty."[19] She recognized that even in our crowded cities, many people are dying of loneliness. This spiritual and emotional poverty can be just as devastating as material poverty.

THREE BARRIERS TO HEALTHY RELATIONSHIPS

If relationships are so vital, why do we struggle with them? Why do we find ourselves acting more like isolated porcupines than connected, living stones?

Let's explore three common barriers that can keep us from experiencing the fullness of healthy relationships.

Barrier 1: Independence at All Costs

In our culture, we prize independence. We celebrate the self-made individual, the lone wolf who doesn't need anyone else. But this mindset is dangerous to relationships and, frankly, is distinctly un-Christian.

The truth is God didn't create us to be independent. He created us to be dependent on Him and interdependent with each other. The apostle Paul puts it beautifully in 1 Corinthians 12:18–19: "But now God has set the members, each one of them,

---

[19] Mother Teresa. In Ratcliffe, S. (Ed.), Oxford Essential Quotations. Oxford University Press. Retrieved 26 Nov. 2024, from https://www.oxfordreference.com/view/10.1093/acref/9780191843730.001.0001/q-oro-ed5-00010799.

in the body, just as He pleased. And if they were all one member, where would the body be?"

We are meant to need each other. Your strengths complement my weaknesses, and vice versa. When we embrace this interdependence, we open ourselves up to the richness of community God intended for us. Think about it like this—when God works in one of us, He works in all of us!

The antidote to independence at all costs is humility. It's recognizing that we don't have all the answers, that we need others in our lives. For me, this looks like having a loving family, close friends, trusted advisors, and pastoral voices I rely on. I'm not perfect, but deciding to walk with others helps me become a better person.

Humility allows us to receive from others, to learn from them, to be shaped by community. It's the recognition we are part of something bigger than ourselves. As Rick Warren put it, "Humility is not thinking less of yourself; it's thinking of yourself less."[20]

Barrier 2: Insecurity at Every Turn

Insecurity is a sneaky barrier to healthy relationships. It whispers lies to us: "You're not good enough." "No one really likes you."

---

[20] Rick Warren, *The Purpose Driven Life: What on Earth Am I Here For?* (Grand Rapids: Zondervan, 2002), 149.

"If they knew the real you, they'd reject you." These thoughts drive us into seclusion, making us "unbondable" with others.

Maybe you've been burned. You trusted someone, opened your heart, and they betrayed you. Now, insecurity tells you that if one person hurt you, anyone could…and everyone will. So you batten down the hatches, push everyone away, and run for the hills.

The antidote to insecurity is honesty. It's being real about our weaknesses, our struggles, our fears. It's finding safe people—a family member, a small group leader, a pastor, a trusted friend, a wise advisor—and opening up to them. Remember, you're only as sick as your secrets. When we bring things into the light, they lose their power over us.

> *The antidote to insecurity is honesty.*

This kind of vulnerability can be scary, but it's also liberating. When we're honest about our struggles, we often find others can relate. Our openness gives them permission to be real, as well. This is how deep, meaningful connections are forged.

I've experienced this in my own life. There was a time when I felt I perpetually had to "have it all together." The pressure of maintaining that façade was exhausting. It was only when I started being honest about my challenges with friends and mentors that I began to experience true freedom and deeper relationships.

Barrier 3: Isolation for the Long Haul

When we give in to independence and insecurity, we often end up in isolation. Proverbs 18:1 warns us about this: "A man who isolates himself seeks his own desire; He rages against all wise judgment."

Isolation is dangerous because it's the incubator for deception. When we're alone with our thoughts, it's easy for lies to take root and grow. The enemy's goal is to get us isolated, because that's where we're most vulnerable.

If the enemy's goal is isolation, God's goal is connection. God wants us surrounded by a community of believers who can encourage us, challenge us, and support us. Think of elephants—they often move in herds, protecting the young and the weak. The power is in the herd. *We are stronger together.*

The antidote to isolation is to help someone else. Take your eyes off yourself. Step out of your comfort zone. If you're hurting, find someone who's hurting worse and help them. Serve, encourage, reach out. It's amazing how our own problems shrink when we focus on helping others.

This principle is beautifully illustrated in the life of Viktor Frankl, a psychiatrist who survived the Nazi concentration camps. In his book *Man's Search for Meaning*, Frankl observed that those who maintained a sense of purpose and connection to others were more likely to survive horrific conditions.[21] Even in the darkest circumstances, reaching out to help others gave people a reason to keep going.

Frankl's insights have been corroborated by numerous studies on resilience in extreme circumstances. For instance, research on POWs from the Vietnam War found that those who maintained strong social bonds and a sense of shared purpose were better able to withstand the trauma of captivity and had better long-term mental health outcomes.[22]

This example underscores a profound truth: human connection isn't just a nice addition to our lives—it's a crucial factor in our ability to survive and thrive, especially in challenging circumstances. When we reach out to others and build and maintain strong relationships, we're not just enriching our lives—we're creating a resilience that can carry us through even the darkest of times.

Thriving relationships fill our tank, increasing our capacity to respond well to adversity. Similarly, if we're operating from a

---

[21] Viktor Frankel. *Man's Search for Meaning.* (Pocket Books, 1997).

[22] Francine Segovia et al., "Optimism Predicts Resilience in Repatriated Prisoners of War: A 37-Year Longitudinal Study," *Journal of Traumatic Stress* 25, no. 3 (2012): 330–336. https://doi.org/10.1002/jts.21691.

relational deficit, it's much more challenging to handle life's ups and downs.

We were born to connect.

PRACTICAL STEPS FOR PURSUING HEALTHY RELATIONSHIPS

Now that we've identified these barriers, let's talk about some practical steps we can take to pursue and build healthy relationships.

1. Be intentional. Relationships don't happen by accident.

We need to be proactive in seeking others out. Reach out to that neighbor you've been meaning to get to know. Join a small group at church. Invite a coworker to lunch. Set aside time in your schedule specifically for nurturing relationships.

2. Be vulnerable. Real relationships require authenticity.

This doesn't mean sharing all of your struggles with everyone you meet, but it does mean being willing to let your guard down with trusted individuals. Share your struggles, your fears, your hopes. Remember, vulnerability is a two-way street—be a safe person for others to open up to as well.

3. Be a servant, just like Jesus modeled for us.

Look for ways to serve others without expecting anything in return. This could be as simple as remembering someone's birthday or offering to help with a project. When we serve, we shift our focus from our own needs to the needs of others, which paradoxically often meets our own needs in the process.

4. Be forgiving. Relationships involve imperfect people (you included).

Real relationships mean there will be hurt and misunderstanding. Choose to forgive quickly and thoroughly. As Ephesians 4:32 reminds us: "Be kind and compassionate to one another, forgiving each other, just as in Christ God forgave you" (NIV). Forgiveness doesn't mean pretending the hurt didn't happen; it means choosing to release the offender from the debt you feel they owe you.

5. Make the first move. Don't wait for others to reach out to you.

Be an initiator. As Proverbs 18:24 tells us, "A man who has friends must himself be friendly, but there is a friend who sticks closer than a brother." This might feel uncomfortable at first, especially if you're introverted or have been hurt in the past. Yet remember, everyone is fighting their own battles. Your initiative might be exactly what someone else needs.

6. Practice active listening. Lean in when others speak.

In our fast-paced world, truly listening to someone is becoming a rare skill. When you're in conversation, focus on understanding rather than just waiting for your turn to speak. Ask follow-up questions. Show genuine interest in what the other person is saying.

7. Cultivate empathy. Put yourself in others' shoes.

Psychologically, empathy is the ability to understand and feel what someone else is feeling. It builds bridges of understanding and deepens our connections. Empathy allows us to respond with compassion first, rather than judgment—something Jesus masterfully demonstrated throughout His ministry. Empathy seeks first to understand, rather than to be understood.

8. Embrace differences. God's family is beautifully designed.

Seek out relationships with people who are different from you in background, culture, and perspective. These relationships can broaden our horizons and help us grow in unexpected ways. Plus, Heaven is the most unique place you'll ever find, with people from every nation, tribe, and tongue as your forever-neighbors.[23]

---

[23] Revelation 7:9. "After these things I looked, and behold, a great multitude which no one could number, of all nations, tribes, peoples, and tongues, standing before the throne and before the Lamb, clothed with white robes, with palm branches in their hands."

THE GOLDEN RULE IN RELATIONSHIPS

Jesus gave us the ultimate principle for healthy relationships in what we call the Golden Rule: "Do to others as you would have them do to you."[24] This simple yet profound guideline can transform our interactions.

One practical application of this is to be more *interested* than *interesting*. We often enter conversations eager to share our own stories, experiences, and opinions. But what if we flipped the script? What if we entered each interaction genuinely curious about the other person?

I love to think about relationships in terms of deposits and withdrawals. Every time we listen actively, show genuine interest, and offer encouragement, we're making a deposit in that relationship. When we need support or have to make a request, we're making a withdrawal. The key is to ensure we're making more deposits than withdrawals.

This principle applies in all areas of life—in our marriage, our friendships, our work relationships, even our interactions with acquaintances. When we consistently treat others the way we want to be treated, we create an atmosphere of mutual respect and care.

---

[24] Luke 6:31. "And just as you want men to do to you, you also do to them likewise."

There's a principle called "social capital" that perfectly illustrates this. It was popularized by a sociologist named Robert Putnam in his book *Bowling Alone*. Putnam's ideas will strike a chord with you.

He argues that the connections we have with each other—our friendships, our involvement in the community, even casual interactions with neighbors—are a kind of wealth. Just like financial capital, this "social capital" can be invested and grown, benefiting both individuals and whole communities.

The disconcerting thing Putnam found is that social capital has been declining in America since the 1950s. Fewer people are joining clubs, volunteering, or even just hanging out with neighbors. He even points to the decline of bowling leagues as an example (hence the book's quirky title).

Now, why does this matter?

Well, Putnam's research shows that communities with high social capital tend to have lower crime rates, better schools, and even better public health. On a personal level, people with strong social networks find jobs more easily, get promoted more often, and even live longer.[25]

---

[25] Robert D. Putnam. *Bowling Alone: The Collapse and Revival of American Community.* (New York: Simon & Schuster, 2020).

Isn't that interesting? It really drives home the point that when we invest in relationships, we're not just making our own lives better. We're actually contributing to the health of our faith and local communities.

Sounds a lot like Jesus's intentions for His disciples in John 13:34–35: "A new commandment I give to you, that you love one another; as I have loved you, that you also love one another. By this all will know that you are My disciples, if you have love for one another."

I saw social capital in action firsthand in the 1990s. I had the privilege of starting an organization called Next Generation. We established student-initiated Bible clubs on junior high and high school campuses throughout the Gulf Coast region.

The kids involved in these clubs weren't just growing spiritually—they were building a network of meaningful relationships that enhanced every aspect of their lives. They excelled in school, developed stronger social networks, and gained a sense of purpose beyond their years.

Conversely, I witnessed that kids who remained isolated and detached from support groups like Next Generation often fared poorly. They faced more challenges in school, battled loneliness, and seemed to lack the resilience that comes from being part of a caring group.

This experience brought Putnam's research to life for me. I saw how investing in relationships could transform not just someone's life, but whole peer groups.

Through Next Generation clubs, we created spaces where students could practice the Golden Rule and experience the power of genuine community.

Next Generation showed me that when we invest in others, we contribute to both our own health and that of our relational network.

OVERCOMING THE LONELINESS EPIDEMIC

Despite our ultra-connected world, loneliness has reached epidemic proportions. We can have hundreds of online friends and still feel profoundly alone. This is where the church—the family of God—has a crucial role to play.

When I was in college, I experienced the healing power of genuine community firsthand. Like many of us, growing up I experienced hurt in different relationships. After I came to Christ, the church became a lifeline for me. It was there I found pastors, mentors, friends, and a sense of belonging that helped shape me into the man I am today.

The church is the place where the lonely find family, where the wounded find healing, where the outcast finds home.

This doesn't happen automatically—it requires intentional effort from all of us. We need to be willing to open our homes, our lives, and our hearts to others.

If you're feeling lonely, I want to encourage you—there is hope. God has a place for you in His family. It might take some courage to step out, to be vulnerable, to risk connection. But I promise you, it's worth it.

BALANCING RELATIONSHIPS AND BOUNDARIES

As we pursue healthy relationships, it's important to acknowledge that not all of them are healthy. While we want to be open and loving, we also need to be wise.

Be cautious of unhealthy relationships that consistently drain you or pull you away from God's best for your life. Surround yourself with people who, as I like to say, add and multiply to your life rather than subtract and divide.

Setting boundaries is not unloving—in fact, it's essential for maintaining healthy relationships. Jesus Himself set boundaries. He often withdrew to be alone with the Father. He didn't allow others' expectations to dictate His actions. He spoke truth, even when it was difficult.

Learning to say "no" to some things allows us to say a wholehearted "yes" to that which truly matters. It's about stewarding our time, energy, and emotional resources.

THE UNDENIABLE POWER OF HEALTHY RELATIONSHIPS

If you remember one thing from this chapter, remember this: You were born to connect, but connection is a decision. Despite your fears, your insecurities, your past hurts—God placed a unique desire within you to connect with Him and others.

Choosing to pursue healthy relationships isn't always easy. It requires vulnerability, intentionality, and sometimes, a willingness to be uncomfortable. But the rewards are immeasurable. When we find our place in God's family, we experience a richness of life that can't be found any other way.

You were born to connect, but connection is a decision.

That reminds me of a single mother in our church. Prior to coming to Christ, she found herself craving love and attention in all the wrong places. As a single mom, she struggled to find community, acceptance, or worthiness. But once she turned to Jesus and discovered her unique place in God's family, she began walking in the truth of who she is in Christ and the purpose God has for her. Today, she is leading her children and other single moms in God's truth while providing community, love, and support.

Remember, you're not a porcupine. You're a living stone, designed to be fitted together with others to create something beautiful. So, let's *decide to thrive* by pursuing healthy relationships. Reach out. Be real. Love and be loved. That's what we were made for.

Reflect

Take some time to process these questions, either in personal reflection or with others in your small group. Growth happens best in community, but honest individual reflection is essential for lasting change.

1. Last week's action step was to build a daily habit of connecting with God. How has that practice been for you throughout the week?

2. How would you describe your current relationships? Are they adding to your life or draining you?

3. Which of the three barriers (independence, insecurity, isolation) do you struggle with most? What's one step you can take this week to overcome that barrier?

4. Who is someone you can build a godly relationship with?

5. How can you be more intentional about being part of a church family? If you're not part of a church community, what's holding you back?

6. Reflect on a time when someone's vulnerability allowed you to open up. How can you create that space for others in your life?

Act

This week, make an effort to pursue a friendship with someone who has a relationship with God. Connect with them throughout your week or reach out to them to grab coffee. In every conversation, try to ask more questions, and be more interested than interesting.

Remember, small steps taken consistently lead to big changes. You don't have to revolutionize your social life overnight. Start where you are, with what you have. Trust that as you step out in faith, God will meet you there.

Pray

Heavenly Father, thank You for creating us for connection. Thank You for the gift of relationships. Help me to overcome my fears and insecurities and give me the courage to pursue healthy relationships. Show me my place in Your family and help me be a blessing to others. Give me wisdom to set healthy boundaries and grace to forgive when I'm hurt. May my relationships reflect Your love to the world. In Jesus's name. Amen.

CHAPTER 4

DECISION 3:
THE PURPOSE DECISION

I CHOOSE TO REACH PEOPLE FOR CHRIST

"Beam me up, Scotty!"

Now there's a phrase that's become part of our cultural DNA, right? For those who might not know, it's the catchphrase from the original *Star Trek* television series. Scrambling on a black-and-white screen, Captain Kirk would use it to ask Chief Engineer Scotty to teleport him to safety aboard the starship *Enterprise*.

Compared to the flashy reboots we've got now, it was practically cardboard and tin foil. Yet the teleporting idea always stuck with me—and millions of others. The idea of instantly zapping from danger to safety (or from home to the grocery store) is appealing. When I came to Christ, though, this funny little phrase took on a new dynamic. I was on fire to serve Jesus and reach people. Yet I couldn't help but think how amazing it'd be if God could beam me up right then to my Heavenly home.

No more pain. No more heartache. No more toil. In a flash, we could be in Heaven itself.

The apostle Paul, while under house arrest in Rome, wrote about a similar feeling, saying in Philippians 1:23–24, "For I am hard-pressed between the two, having a desire to depart and be with Christ, which is far better. Nevertheless to remain in the flesh is more needful for you."

Paul shows us we aren't saved just for our own benefit. We are saved to be part of God's grand plan to reach others with His love. Which is why he continued in verses 25 and 26:

And being confident of this, I know that I shall remain and continue with you all for your progress and joy of faith, that your rejoicing for me may be more abundant in Jesus Christ by my coming to you again.

Friends, that's what this life is ultimately about. Make the next decision for a thriving life: **The Purpose Decision**. This means embracing that, in Christ, your life *isn't just about you*. God's design isn't to save you and immediately beam you up to Heaven. He leaves you here on Earth for a purpose.

You were made for more.

I remember a pivotal moment in my own journey when this truth really hit home. A number of years ago, a mentor of mine shared his personal goal of leading a certain number of people to Christ every year.

I thought, Wow! That is a person who understands his purpose is to make an impact in people's lives for eternity.

That is the purpose I invite you to discover and embrace. To pause and really think, "Does my life reflect the God-given purpose of reaching people for Christ?"

In some ways, it probably does. In other ways, it'll be time for some refocusing. Wherever you are in life, know this: The adventure begins when you choose to reach people for Christ, no matter what it takes. *That* is what the Purpose Decision is all about.

To start, what is purpose?

UNDERSTANDING OUR PURPOSE

Do you remember the last time you met someone new? They probably thought, "So, what do you do?" Perhaps you even asked them. Our job often jumps to the top of the list. In our culture, our worth is often tied to our work.

You may answer your new acquaintance, "I'm a businessperson…"

"I'm a student…"

"I'm an electrician…"

"I'm a [fill in the blank]…"

You see, there's a big difference between your job (vocation) and God's purpose for you (calling). This can be a hard thing to sift through. However, before we dive into Jesus's Great Commission for us to go reach people and make disciples, you have to understand this.

Your job title probably isn't "evangelist." Yet you are called to evangelize.

Your job title probably isn't "pastor." Yet you are called to care for others.

Your job title probably isn't "missionary." Yet you walk onto your mission field every day (i.e. your workplace, school campus, local gym), talking to people who don't know Christ.

You eventually retire from your vocation, but never from your purpose. God uses your job to fulfill your purpose, but He elevates your purpose above your job—because your purpose never stops. Never forget, as long as you have a pulse, you have a purpose. Every single one of us who follows Jesus is called to lead people to Him.

God has strategically placed you exactly where you are for a reason. Your job, your neighborhood, your hobbies—these aren't just random circumstances. They're divine opportunities. They're chances to shine Christ's light on those who may never darken the doors of a church.

God uses our vocations to position us in places to lead people to Christ. The person you work with… the neighbor you chat with…the barista who makes your coffee… God has put all these people in your path for a purpose.

To fully commit to the Purpose Decision, we must grasp the real gravity of our situation. The Bible paints a sobering picture of humanity's condition apart from

> *As long as you have a pulse, you have a purpose.*

Christ. Ephesians 2:1 tells us that we are "…dead in trespasses and sins." Remember, Romans 3:23 tells us: "For all have sinned and fall short of the glory of God."

This isn't just religious talk—it's the reality of our human condition. We live in a sin-broken world. People seek meaning and purpose in all the wrong places. Brokenness, addiction, and disconnection are rising rapidly in our society. They all point to a deeper, spiritual need.

We must know that humanity's deepest need is spiritual—not mental, physical, or emotional. These areas are important and often linked, yet fixing only the surface issues is like putting a Band-Aid on a broken bone. It doesn't address the root problem. People need more than positive thinking and behavior change. They need the gospel's transformative power in the human heart.

This is where Christ comes in. He is the ultimate solution to humanity's deepest need. He offers forgiveness, reconciliation with God, and a purpose greater than ourselves. We, as believers, have been entrusted with this life-changing message and mission.

OVERCOMING BARRIERS TO SHARING OUR FAITH

Now, I know that sharing our faith doesn't always come easily. Let's address some of the barriers head-on:

Fear and insecurity: It's normal to feel nervous about sharing your faith. "What if they reject me? What if I don't know enough?" It's not about your eloquence and ability to communicate. It's about simply sharing the life-changing love of Christ and your personal story.

Lack of knowledge: You don't need a theology degree to share your faith. Start with what you do know—your own story of how Christ has changed your life. At the same time, it's important to be prepared. As 1 Peter 3:15 reminds us, we should always be ready to give a "reason for the hope" that we have.[26] You don't need to be an expert in apologetics. But be thoughtful about your faith and why you believe it. There are many resources available to read, watch, or listen to.

Misconceptions about evangelism: Some think evangelism is just the image of the street preacher with a megaphone. An effective way to evangelize is through sharing the Good News in genuine relationships and conversations. You don't have to be an evangelist like Billy Graham, who preached to thousands, to share your faith with the people in your life.

The key is to find the right balance between our "walk" and our "talk." Our lives should reflect Christ's love. But we must also share the reason for our hope.

YOUR TESTIMONY IS POWERFUL

One of the most powerful tools we have in reaching others is our personal testimony (or, your God-story). John the Revelator tells us in Revelation 12:11 that we overcome "…by the blood of the Lamb and by the word of [our] testimony…" Your story of how Jesus has changed your life is your unique testimony–and it's powerful.

I remember a time in my own life when I felt lost and without purpose. In college, the reality and pain of my sin caught up with me. My mistakes mounted, and the burden of my guilt crushed me. It was then that I started seeking Jesus. But I realized He'd been seeking me all along. When I realized that Jesus came for the sick, for sinners like me, I surrendered my life to Christ and

---

[26] 1 Peter 3:15. "But sanctify the Lord God in your hearts, and always be ready to give a defense to everyone who asks you a reason for the hope that is in you, with meekness and fear."

went all in. My only reasonable response was to give Him my whole life in that Bible study my freshman year in college.

Your story might be different. Maybe you grew up in the church but had a moment when your faith became real and personal. Or, you hit rock bottom and found Christ was there to pick you up. Whatever your story, it has the power to connect with someone who needs to hear it.

PRACTICAL STEPS FOR REACHING PEOPLE

We must adopt a lifestyle that practically engages with others around us. Let me share a few key principles.

First, **bear some burdens**.

In Mark 2, we see four guys determined to bring their paralyzed friend to Jesus. The house where Jesus was teaching was so crowded they couldn't get in. Yet they didn't give up. They climbed up on the roof made of beams covered with thatch and mud. Then they dug through it and lowered their friend down through the hole in the roof to Jesus!

This story shows us that evangelism can be a team sport. It wasn't just one guy, but a group working together to help their friend. Plus, it reminds us that, sometimes, reaching people for Jesus can get messy. At times we have to dig through some "mud" in people's lives, but it's worth it to see them transformed.

Second, **do whatever it takes**.

Just like those friends in Mark 2, we need to be creative and persistent to reach people. We never compromise our values or ethics. But it does mean stepping out of our comfort zones.

Third, **build a prayer strategy**.

It can be as simple as this: create a list of people you'd love to see come to Christ. Pray for them every day. Ask God to open doors for conversations and to soften their hearts.

Before we move on, take a moment to start your salvation list right now. Write out the names of people you'd love to see come to Jesus.

1. _____

2. _____

3. _____

4. _____

5. _____

Fourth, **watch for opportunities**.

Look for divine opportunities to bring up spiritual topics. It could be as simple as asking someone if there's any way you can pray for them.

While I was in seminary, I waited tables. One of the guys I worked with constantly told me he was "spiritual" and could sense positive and negative energy. However, he wasn't a Christian. That gave me a daily assignment to pray for an opportunity to talk to him about Jesus. One day after work it happened—I had the privilege to lead him to Christ.

It really is that simple. Pray that you would see opportunities to share Christ with hurting people. I have never known God to leave that prayer unanswered.

Just like those four friends in Mark 2, our ultimate goal is to bring people into an encounter with Jesus. This might mean inviting them to have coffee or grab lunch with you. It might mean inviting them to church or sharing a Bible verse that's meaningful to you. It could also be telling them how Jesus has impacted your life.

THE HOLY SPIRIT IS ALWAYS WORKING

Yes, we're stepping out to reach others. But remember we're not doing this alone. In Acts 1:8, Jesus promises we will receive power when the Holy Spirit comes upon us. That power will equip us to be Christ's witnesses.

The Greek word for power is *dunamis*, from which we get our English word "dynamite." It's not just a little boost. It's supernatural dynamite. The Holy Spirit can break through the hardest hearts and reshape the world around you.

As we rely on the Holy Spirit, He will give us boldness to push through our fears, insecurities, and inhibitions. He will also guide our conversations. He'll give us the right words and work in the hearts of those we're reaching out to. Our job is simply to be available and obedient. The results are up to God.

One area I'm particularly passionate about is reaching the next generation. Studies have shown that the majority of people who come to Christ do so between the ages of four and fourteen.[27] This "4–14 window" is a crucial time for evangelism and discipleship.

Parents, you have a great opportunity and a responsibility. You can lead your children to Christ. Make it a priority in your home. I highly recommend the book *Leading Your Child to Christ* by Andrew Murray. It's great for parents wanting to guide their children to faith in Christ.

A BIG MISSION WITH BIGGER URGENCY

Now, let's not forget this mission should create a fire-in-the-bones urgency within us. Every moment, people are making eternal decisions. Sharing the gospel takes a moment, but it impacts people forever.

I'm reminded of a story I once heard about an old Australian man. He had shared his faith for decades, but only led one

---

[27] George Barna, *Transforming Children into Spiritual Champions* (Baker Books, 2013).

person to faith. For years, he felt like a failure. What he didn't know was that the one person he led to Christ became a powerful evangelist who led thousands to the Lord. The old man only found out about his impact at the very end of his life.

This story reminds us we may never see the full impact of our evangelistic efforts in this lifetime. Just as a tree may never see the forest grown from its seeds, you may never see the fruit from the seeds that you've planted. But each one we planted is working below the surface, even if it takes time to come forth. The gospel's power is exponential and will multiply in due time.

NOT EASY BUT WORTH IT

Living out this daily decision isn't always easy. We don't reap every seed we plant, but it's our job to plant the seeds. There are many challenges:

1. **Comfort zones and complacency:** Comfort is one of the most subtle idols in our culture today. Too often we go *out of our way* to stay comfortable. But reaching people for Christ requires discomfort. It means listening to the promptings of the Holy Spirit to pray for someone.

2. **Rejection and discouragement:** Here's the truth, friend. Not everyone will respond positively to the gospel. That can be gut-wrenching–especially when you've prayed, served,

shown up, been faithful, and partnered with God at every turn. Here's a helpful way to think about it. No doesn't mean "never;" it just means "not yet."

3. **"Ugly orthodoxy":** Francis Schaeffer coined this term.[28] It describes the mindset of knowing the truth but not sharing it. Imagine you see a group of people happily drifting down a river. Yet they're unaware of the waterfall they're about to plummet down. Would it be inconvenient to get your shoes muddy running to warn them? Sure. Would you have any hesitation to save them? No way! Friends, the gospel is *the* message that impacts people's eternal destiny.

We must focus on Jesus and our mission's eternal worth to overcome these obstacles. Yes, it may be uncomfortable at times. But the joy of seeing someone come to Christ far outweighs any discomfort.

LIVING OUT OUR PURPOSE

To reach others for Christ, we need to move from beliefs to behavior. It's not enough to just profess our values; we must live them. Our actions should match our beliefs. They should show our faith to others.

This is where the difference between serving, influence, and evangelism comes into play. Serving and influence are

---

[28] Francis A. Schaeffer, "Two Contents, Two Realities," in *The Complete Works of Francis A. Schaeffer*, vol. 3 (Westchester, IL: Crossway Books, 1982), 416.

important—they help us value people, gain credibility, and build relationships. Yet they're not the end goal. The end goal is ultimately to lead people to Christ.

Don't forget, 1 Peter 3:15 says: "Always be prepared to give an answer to everyone who asks you to give the reason for the hope that you have" (NIV). We should be ready to share and explain our faith. (This is called apologetics.) Notice that this comes in the context of people asking us about our hope. Our lives should be so transformed by Christ that people can't help but notice and want to know more.

As we faithfully reach others, we also find joy. A deep satisfaction comes from knowing we're aligned with God's will for our lives. Nothing compares to the thrill of seeing someone embrace Christ. Their life changes as a result. Leading someone to Christ impacts their eternal destiny, not just their life on Earth. Our main motivation should be our love for God and others.

MAKE THE PURPOSE DECISION TODAY

I want to encourage you to make a decision today. Will you embrace your purpose to share Christ with others? Will you commit to intentionally pray for opportunities to share your faith and lead others to Christ?

This doesn't mean you have to quit your job and become a full-time evangelist. It means living with an awareness of your divine purpose in whatever sphere God has placed you. It means being ready to share the hope you have in Christ. It means seeing every interaction as a potential opportunity to shine Christ's light and love.

Remember, it's important to see your job or vocation as a tool that brings you into spaces and places others can't go. God uses that tool to reach people for Christ. In 2 Corinthians 5:20, Paul says we become "ambassadors" for Christ, joining God's mission to reconcile the world to Himself through Christ.

As you make this decision, I encourage you to bathe it in prayer. Ask God to give you His heart for the lost. Ask Him to open your eyes to the opportunities around you. Ask Him for the courage and wisdom to step out in faith.

Reflect

Take some time to process these questions, either in personal reflection or with others in your small group. Growth happens best in community, but honest individual reflection is essential for lasting change.

1. Last week's action step was to grow in godly relationships. How has that practice been for you throughout the week? Have you noticed a difference in your relationships?

2. Who are three to five people in your sphere of influence who need to know Christ? Commit to praying for them daily.

3. What's your story of how Christ has changed your life? Practice sharing it in two or three minutes.

4. What's one step you can take this week to create an opportunity to share Christ with someone?

5. How can you get more involved in your church's outreach efforts?

6. If you're a parent, how can you be more intentional about leading your children to Christ?

7. What is holding you back from sharing your faith with others? How can you overcome this?

Act

Remember, you were born for this purpose. Jesus saved you to lead others to Himself! Start praying for one person you see regularly who doesn't know Jesus. Ask God for the chance to share your faith with them.

Pray

Heavenly Father, thank You for the great privilege of partnering with You to reach others for Christ. Give me Your heart for the lost. Help me to see people as You see them. Fill me with Your spirit and empower me to be Your witness. Give me courage to step out of my comfort zone and wisdom to share Your love effectively. Use me, Lord, to impact lives for eternity. In Jesus's name. Amen.

CHAPTER 5

DECISION 4:
THE GROWTH DECISION

I CHOOSE TO GROW DAILY AND
HELP OTHERS DO THE SAME

HAVE YOU EVER felt like you're running on the treadmill of life? You're expending a ton of energy, but you're not going anywhere. Maybe you look at your life and wonder, "Is this as good as it gets?"

I get it. I've been there. So have many others. The truth is—God didn't create you to live stuck. He created you to grow, to thrive, and to become more like Him every day. In 2 Peter 3:18, we're called to "…grow in the grace and knowledge of our Lord and Savior Jesus Christ." God's design for your life isn't stagnation—it's transformation. You were born to grow.

In this chapter, we're going to dive deep into what it means to make **The Growth Decision**. We'll explore why growth is essential, what holds us back, and how we can partner with God in order to thrive in life. But here's the key: *the greatest way* *to grow personally is to help others grow!* It's about becoming a disciple of Jesus and helping others become disciples as well.

GOD'S DESIGN FOR GROWTH

Let's talk about how God designed us. In 1 Thessalonians 5:23, Paul writes, "Now may the God of peace Himself sanctify you completely; and may your whole spirit, soul, and body be preserved blameless at the coming of our Lord Jesus Christ." Paul writes that we're body, soul, and spirit. But what does that really mean?

Think of it like this: your spirit is the core of who you are. It's the part that connects directly with God. Your soul includes your mind, will, and emotions. And your body? Well, that's the physical part we can all see, which connects to our environment through our five senses.

Before you become a Christian, the Bible says you're dead in your trespasses and sins.[29] When you become a Christian, your spirit comes alive. It's like flipping on a light switch in a dark room. Suddenly, everything is different. But here's the catch: your soul—your thoughts, feelings, and decisions—still need to be renewed. It's used to being in charge, and it's got some old habits that die hard.

This is where growth comes in. God wants your spirit, now alive and connected to Him, to start influencing and leading your soul and body. **He wants every part of your life to thrive.**

I remember when I first became a Christian. Man, I thought I'd instantly have it all together. Spoiler alert: I didn't. Quickly, I realized growth is a process, not a one-time event.

It's like planting a seed. When you plant an apple seed, you don't expect a full-grown tree overnight, right? Of course not! It takes time, water, sunlight, and the right conditions for that seed to grow into a thriving, fruitful apple tree.

The same is true for us. 1 Peter 2:2 says, "Like newborn babies, crave pure spiritual milk, so that by it you may grow up in your salvation" (NIV). We start as spiritual infants, where we're still largely controlled by our thoughts, will, feelings, and impulses.

---

[29] Ephesians 2:5. "even when we were dead in trespasses, made us alive together with Christ (by grace you have been saved)."

But God's plan is for us to grow into mature believers where we're led by the Word of God and the Holy Spirit within us.

Let's never forget—healthy things grow. The same is true for us spiritually. God's design for your life isn't to stay the same year after year. He wants you to keep changing and growing in both your relationship with Jesus and in His character.

HOW DO YOU CHANGE?

Did you know your soul is the control center for your life? It's true. The way you think shapes your emotions, your decisions, and your actions. That's why it's so important that you to thrive.

Paul tells us in Romans 12:2, "Do not conform to the pattern of this world, but be transformed by the renewing of your mind" (NIV). This verse is crucial for understanding Christian growth, which is called discipleship.

When I first read Romans 12:2, I thought, "Sounds great, but how exactly do I do that?"

Here's the thing: renewing your mind is an ongoing process. It's about consistently replacing old, sinful, unhelpful thought patterns with new ones that align with God's truth.

Our thoughts create feelings → that drive decisions → which lead to actions → which determine our outcomes.

Think of your mind as a garden. The thoughts you allow to take root will determine the "fruit" your life produces. If you let weeds of negativity, doubt, and fear grow wild, that's what your life will show. If you intentionally plant and nurture thoughts of faith, hope, and love, that's what will flourish in your life.

This renewal process impacts every area of our lives. It changes how we view God, ourselves, and others. It also affects how we make decisions, handle stress, and face challenges. Remember you are made in the image of God, and you have the power to decide the thoughts you dwell on. Like Martin Luther, the famous reformer, said: "You cannot keep birds from flying over your head, but you can keep them from building a nest in your hair."[30]

Our thoughts create feelings → that drive decisions → which lead to actions → which determine our outcomes.

You have the power to keep your hair nest-free!

I remember when I first started applying this principle. I had a habit of negative self-talk. Whenever I made a mistake, my go-to

[30] Martin Luther, *Luther's Catechetical Writings: God's Call to Repentance, Faith, and Prayer*, trans. John Nicholas Lenker (Minneapolis: National Lutheran Library Association, 1907), 305.

thought was, "I'm such an idiot." Not exactly the most uplifting thought, right?

But as I began to renew my mind with God's Word, I started catching those thoughts and replacing them with truth. Instead of "I'm an idiot," I'd think and say, "I made a mistake, but I'm learning and growing." It might seem like a small change, but over time, it completely transformed how I viewed myself and how I approached challenges.

Now, here's where many of us miss the mark regarding growth. We get comfortable. We find a nice, cozy comfort zone, and set up camp there. But comfort zones, while they feel safe, are often growth killers.

It's like a boat in a harbor. A harbor is a great place for a boat to rest, to refuel, and to prepare for what's next. But that's not where boats are meant to stay forever. Boats are made for the open sea, for adventure, and for new destinations. If a boat never leaves the harbor, it's not fulfilling its purpose.

In the same way, God didn't design you to stay comfortable. He designed you to grow, to be transformed, and to thrive. That means leaving the safety of the harbor and venturing into unknown waters. One of the ways we cling to safety is by clinging to our old thoughts, feelings, words, and actions. Paul said in Ephesians 4:22–24 we are to "put off" our old selves and "put on" our new selves.

So, practically, how do we grow in discipleship through renewing our minds? Here are a few key decisions:

1. Decide to saturate your mind with God's Word.

2. Decide to declare and speak God's truth over your life.

3. Decide to be aware of your thoughts and notice what's going on in your mind.

4. Decide to challenge thoughts that don't align with God's truth.

5. Decide to replace negative thoughts with positive, biblical ones.

6. Decide to surround yourself with people who encourage your growth.

Remember, this is a process. It takes time. Sometimes it will seem like you are taking one step forward and two steps back. But as you consistently renew your mind, you'll start to see transformation in your life as a follower of Jesus Christ.

OBSTACLES TO GROWTH

Now, let's get real for a moment. Growth isn't always easy. In fact, sometimes it's an all-out war. Why? There's a battle going on inside each of us.

The first and perhaps biggest obstacle to growth is **trying to grow alone**. This lesson I learned the hard way. I played sports in high school and consistently worked out. After high school

I continued to work out, but never as rigorously as when I was playing football. It wasn't until a few years ago, when I got a trainer, someone who held me accountable, that I really started pressing in again with weight training. There's something about another person helping you on your journey that makes you better.

The same principle applies to our spiritual growth. We weren't designed to grow alone. We need others to encourage us, challenge us, and hold us accountable.

Here are some other common obstacles to growth:

- **Complacency:** It's so easy to get comfortable where we are, isn't it? We find our routine, our familiar habits, and we stick to them like glue. Change? No thanks, we're good here. But remember that boat we talked about? Comfort zones might feel safe, but they're not where real growth happens.

- **Fear:** This is a big one. Fear of failure, fear of the unknown, fear of what others might think. It's like that voice in your head saying, "What if you try, and it doesn't work out? What if you look foolish?" Fear can paralyze us.

- **Past hurts:** Maybe you've been burned before. You trusted someone, opened your heart, and they let you down. Or you tried something new, and it didn't work out. Those experiences can make us hesitant to put ourselves out there again.

- **Lies we believe:** These are those sneaky thoughts that creep in and tell us we'll never measure up, that we'll never change, that God couldn't possibly love us. They're like weeds in our mental garden, choking out the truth if we let them grow.

Remember, these obstacles—trying to grow alone, complacency, fear, past hurts, and lies—they're common to all of us. You're not alone in facing them. The key is recognizing them for what they are: obstacles, not dead ends. With God's help and the support of others, you can overcome and thrive.

PERSONAL GROWTH THROUGH MAKING DISCIPLES

Studies have shown that the greatest way to learn is to teach.

Now that we've talked about becoming a disciple and personal growth, let's shift gears and talk about the second part of our growth decision: **Making Disciples**.

You see, God's plan for our personal growth *also* includes helping others grow. He wants us to take what we've learned and share it with others. This is what we call discipleship, and it's at the heart of one of Jesus's last commands to His followers.

In Matthew 28:19–20, Jesus says, "Go therefore and make disciples of all the nations, baptizing them in the name of the Father and of the Son and of the Holy Spirit, teaching them to observe all things that I have commanded you…"

This isn't just a suggestion—it's a command.

The Greek word for "disciple" (*mathētēs*) means "disciplined learner," which implies there's someone to learn from. You can't be a disciple unless someone is teaching you, and if you *are* a "disciplined learner," you are *doing* what a disciplined learner does. In 1 Corinthians 11:1 Paul says, "Imitate me, just as I also imitate Christ." As Paul explains, discipleship means *being* and *doing* are inseparable. Following Jesus means both *being* a disciple and *doing* what a disciple does—making disciples!

It's part of our purpose as followers of Christ. We're called not just to grow ourselves, but to help others grow.

Studies show that teaching others is one of the best ways to learn.[31] For example, when students explain ideas to their classmates, they understand the material much better than if they just read or listen. This method of learning by teaching helps students think more deeply about the subject. It also makes them more aware of how they learn. One year after becoming a Christian, I was challenged by my Bible study leader to step out and lead a group myself. Although I was nervous at first, I found great joy and fulfillment in leading the group. Why? When I prepared my lesson, I was growing and learning myself. You learn best when you share with others.

---

[31] Erin L. Dolan and James P. Collins, "We Must Teach More Effectively: Here Are Four Ways to Get Started," *Molecular Biolology of the Cell* 15, no. 26 (June 2015): 2151–5. doi: 10.1091/mbc.E13-11-0675.

Now, I know what you might be thinking. "I'm not a pastor or a Bible scholar. How can I make disciples?" Here's the beautiful thing: you don't need to be an expert to help someone else grow. You just need to be one step ahead on the journey.

Think about it like this. If you've been following Christ for a year, you have valuable experience to share with someone who's just starting out. If you've overcome a particular struggle or learned a valuable lesson, that's something you can pass on to others.

You just need to be one step ahead on the journey.

Making disciples isn't about having all the answers. It's about walking alongside others, sharing what you've learned, and pointing them to Christ and His Word. It's about helping someone else grow in their faith and seeing the fulfillment of God's purpose in their life.

Here are some practical ways you can start making disciples:

1. Be intentional about building relationships with other believers— especially those newer to the faith.

2. Offer to study the Bible with someone.

3. Invite them to a small group where biblical topics are discussed.

4. Share experiences and lessons you've learned in your walk with Christ.

5. Be open about your own struggles and how God is helping you grow.

6. Invite others to join you in serving people in your community.

Making disciples literally means to *train* someone in the Scriptures and how to become a follower of Jesus. It brings to mind the intentionality of forming a clay pot. Clay is messy at first—but then it is molded into a beautiful pot. In the same way, discipling people is messy work that takes effort and energy. It involves getting into people's lives, being there for them in their struggles, and sometimes having difficult conversations. Yet it's also incredibly rewarding. There's nothing quite like seeing someone you've invested in grow in their faith and start to make disciples themselves.

> *Growth is the progressive layering of daily choices over time.*

COMPOUND GROWTH

As we've said, decisions create your outcomes in life. We're making thousands of decisions every day. Growth is the progressive layering of daily choices over time.

Think about it like compound interest. If you invest a little every day, over time it adds up to something significant. The same principle applies to our spiritual and personal growth.

I learned this lesson the hard way. Very early in my Christian walk, I thought growth would just happen automatically. I'd go to church on Sunday, feel inspired, and then still struggle to change. The problem was I wasn't making the necessary daily decisions to grow.

It wasn't until I started making intentional decisions each day that I began to see substantial change. For me, that happened when I joined a small group led by a man named Doug. When I made the decision to be part of that small group and to be accountable to others–everything changed. I began to grow as a follower of Jesus. That's what discipleship is all about. I am forever grateful to Doug for pouring into my life and helping me work through all of my muddy mess.

Your daily growth decisions might look different. Maybe it's choosing to wake up earlier to read your Bible and pray. Perhaps it's learning how to forgive someone if they've hurt you. It could also mean choosing to serve in your local church or community. Or even something as simple as listening to a sermon on your drive to work.

The specific decision isn't as important as its consistent practice. God hardwired us for habits. Author James Clear said in his book *Atomic Habits*, "It's hard to change your habits if you never change the underlying beliefs that led to your past behavior."[32] Your decision to create healthy habits will ultimately foster growth and help you thrive.

Here's some good news—your life doesn't have to be overhauled overnight. Set yourself up for success by starting small. I encourage you to try this: Now that you understand what becoming a disciple is, choose one habit that will help you grow. Start implementing the habit. Then make small adjustments each day to keep moving in a positive direction.

Remember the apple seed we talked about earlier? One small seed, planted and nurtured consistently, can grow into a tree that produces thousands of apples. Your small, daily decisions are like that seed. They might not seem like much at the moment, but over time, they have the power to transform your life—and the lives of those around you.

GROWING TOGETHER

As we wrap up, let's revisit our definition of the Growth Decision: *I choose to grow daily and help others do the same.* This isn't just about personal development—it's about growing in your relationship with Christ and helping others do the same.

Remember, growth isn't about perfection. It's about progress. We are called both to make disciples—and be a disciple.

---

[32] James Clear, *Atomic Habits: An Easy & Proven Way to Build Good Habits & Break Bad Ones* (New York: Avery, 2018).

This involves rolling up our sleeves and doing the hard, messy work of investing in others' lives.

As you grow, remember that your growth isn't just for you. It's so you can pour into others, helping them grow in their faith too. That's how we fulfill the Great Commission. That's how we make a lasting impact for God's Kingdom.

Reflect

Take some time to process these questions, either in personal reflection or with others in your small group. Growth happens best in community, but honest individual reflection is essential for lasting change.

Let's take some time to reflect on what we've learned and put it into action. Here are some questions to ponder and steps to take:

1. Last week's action step was to pray for and share your faith with someone who doesn't know Christ. How has that practice been for you throughout the week?

2. In what areas of your life do you feel most stuck right now? What's holding you back from growing in these areas?

3. How can you continually renew your mind to be more aligned with Christ?

4. Which of the obstacles to growth (complacency, fear, past hurts, lies we believe, isolation) do you struggle with most? How has this obstacle affected your growth journey?

5. What is God speaking to you about growing and helping others grow? What steps do you need to take?

6. What fears or doubts do you have about making disciples, and how can you overcome them?

7. Who can you be intentional with in building a relationship that leads to discipleship?

Act

This week, help someone grow in their relationship with God. Think about the people in your life. Is there someone who could use encouragement in their faith journey? Maybe a friend who's struggling with doubt, a family member who's curious about Christianity, or a neighbor who's open to spiritual conversations?

Choose one person and commit to taking a step to help them grow closer to God this week. It could be as simple as sharing a meaningful Bible verse, inviting them to join you in prayer, or having a heartfelt conversation about faith.

Remember, small actions can have a big impact. By consistently investing in others' spiritual growth, week by week, you're planting seeds that can lead to a bountiful harvest in God's Kingdom.

This week, help someone grow in their relationship with God. Who will you choose, and what step will you take?

Pray

Heavenly Father, thank You for Your incredible design for my life. Thank You for creating me to thrive, not just survive. Help me to grow as a follower of Jesus. Give me the courage to make decisions that lead to growth, even when it's uncomfortable. Give me wisdom to surround myself with people who will encourage me and challenge me to keep growing. And most of all, help me to rely on Your strength, not my own, as I press on toward becoming more like Jesus and leading others to do the same. In His name we pray. Amen.

CHAPTER 6

DECISION 5:
THE INFLUENCE DECISION

I CHOOSE TO MAKE A DIFFERENCE THROUGH MY UNIQUE GIFTS, TALENTS, AND ABILITIES

Remember the classic story *A Christmas Carol*? Ebenezer Scrooge was a miserable penny-pincher. All he cared about was his money. In the end, what did that get him? Nothing but loneliness and misery!

Scrooge only had a happy ending when he shifted his focus from self to others. It's a paradox, but it's true: *you find your life by serving others.* That's the life Jesus modeled, which is the next decision in your journey.

> *You find your life by serving others.*

The Influence Decision means choosing to make a difference in the lives of others with who you are.

In a sense, your gifts, talents, and abilities are a lot like Scrooge's money. Scrooge only found real purpose when he stopped hoarding his money and discovered the joy in giving it away. Your abilities and time aren't just for you—they're about how you can serve others and make a difference in this world. When we align our lives with this divine design, something remarkable happens.

We enjoy fulfillment through service.

Paul understood this principle well. In 1 Thessalonians 2:7–8, he writes, "But we were gentle among you, just as a nursing mother cherishes her own children. So, affectionately longing for you, we were well pleased to impart to you not only the gospel of God, but also our own lives, because you had become dear to us."

Paul wasn't just preaching a message; he was giving himself away. He knew true influence comes through caring for and serving people. He didn't think the titles he held made him special. He didn't lord his spiritual position over the Thessalonian people. Instead, he treated them like his own children.

This is the servant leader's playbook.

FLIPPING THE SCRIPT

In Mark 10:37, we get to watch an interesting interaction. Two brothers, the disciples James and John, approached Jesus. They wanted a favor, asking: "Grant us that we may sit, one on Your right hand and the other on Your left, in Your glory."

James and John saw power like the world did. Success to them was about titles, position, and prestige. Just a few verses later, we learn their scheme infuriated the other disciples! Yet, Jesus turned the disagreement into a revolutionary lesson.

In Mark 10:43b–44, He said, "…but whoever desires to become great among you shall be your servant. And whoever of you desires to be first shall be slave of all." Jesus flipped the script on everything they thought they knew about influencing others.

Then, in verse 45, He summed it up this way, "For even the Son of Man did not come to be served, but to serve, and to give His life a ransom for many."

Imagine how different our world would be if we all adopted a servant mindset. It's not just a nice idea; it's a transformative way of living that changes everything.

Now, before you skip this chapter, thinking, "I'm not a leader!" hear me out. The Influence Decision isn't about the job title of leader. It's about serving others right where you are with what you have to offer.

Missionary statesman J. Oswald Sanders says in his book *Spiritual Leadership*, "Leadership is influence." So, if leadership is influence, servant leadership is one of the greatest ways to influence people.[33] When we flip the script and choose to lead through influence, that's called serving people. When we serve others, three amazing things happen:

1. **Personal transformation:** We grow when we serve others. Our character is shaped, our perspective broadens, and we discover a deep sense of purpose and joy.

2. **Church activation:** When believers embrace servant leadership, the Church comes alive. Seeing people's lives change is exciting. There's nothing like being an answer to someone's prayer.

3. **Community impact:** Servant leaders become God's agents of lasting change–from our neighborhoods to our schools to our workplaces and beyond. Every act of God-inspired service creates a ripple effect. Be the stone that gets it started.

We can define servant leadership this way: a servant leader is someone who uses their God-given gifts, talents, and abilities to serve others and influence them for Christ. When we lose ourselves in service to others, we find true fulfillment.

---

[33] Sanders, J. Oswald. *Spiritual Leadership*. (Chicago: Moody Publishers, 2007).

THE POWER OF THE TOWEL

In John 13, it was Jesus's last night on Earth. The next day, He would be crucified—and He knew it.

The disciples are gathered for what will be their last meal together before the cross. What does Jesus do? He gets up from the table, takes off His outer clothing, and wraps a towel around His waist. Then He starts washing His disciples' feet.

Foot-washing was a lowly task in ancient Israel. People wore open-toed sandals, and no paved roads meant lots of dirt and animal waste. It's not hard to imagine why feet got *very* dirty. That's why this job was usually done by the lowest servant in a household.

Yet Jesus, despite being the Son of God and King of kings, chose to kneel down and wash His disciples' filthy feet.

The Savior stooped to do the work of the lowest servant. In God's family, servant leaders kneel.

This moment teaches us five powerful lessons about servant leadership:

1. **Serve from love:** Jesus knew Judas would betray Him. He knew the disciples would soon scatter. Yet, His love for them was unconditional. "Agape" love—God's unconditional love—motivated His service. When we serve others, are we doing it out of genuine love, or for personal recognition?

2. **Confidence empowers others:** In John 13:4 Jesus, "...rose from supper and laid aside His garments, took a towel and girded Himself." He was secure enough to take on a servant's role. Remember, the insecure are into titles; the secure are into towels. Are you secure enough to serve others sacrificially?

3. **Initiative meets real needs:** Jesus saw a practical need—dirty feet—and He met it. No fanfare, no committees, just action. Servant leaders don't wait around; they take initiative. What needs do you see around you that you can meet today?

4. **Courage in the face of rejection:** When Jesus came to Peter, He faced resistance. "You shall never wash my feet!"[34] Peter exclaimed. But Jesus persisted, knowing this act was crucial. Serving others can be awkward and even be met with rejection. Are you willing to push through those uncomfortable moments?

5. **Humility is contagious:** Jesus told His disciples in John 13:15, "For I have given you an example, that you should do as I have done to you." His act of service was contagious. When we serve, it inspires others to do the same. How have you experienced this ripple effect in your own life?

Jesus didn't just talk about servant leadership; He lived it out in tangible, memorable ways. He showed us true greatness isn't about position or power, but about willingness to serve.

---

[34] John 13:8. "Peter said to Him, 'You shall never wash my feet!' Jesus answered him. 'If I do not wash you, you have no part with Me'."

So here's a question to ponder—what's your equivalent of foot-washing today? Where in your life—at home, at work, in your community—can you roll up your sleeves, grab a towel, and serve?

Jesus flipped the script on leadership. Let's wind back the clock and meet King David's best friend to better understand servant leadership.

A CHAMPION OF DREAMS

Do you remember Jonathan from the Old Testament? He was King Saul's son, the heir apparent to Israel's throne. As is often the case, God had other plans. He chose David to be the next king.

How would you react if someone else got the promotion you thought was yours? Bitterness? Jealousy? Not Jonathan. Instead of resenting David, he became his biggest advocate.

1 Samuel 18:1 says, "…the soul of Jonathan was knit to the soul of David, and Jonathan loved him as his own soul." Jonathan gave David his robe. Jonathan saw the big picture beyond his own interests. He recognized God's hand on David's life and aligned himself with God's plan.

Are you willing to set aside your personal ambitions when you see God working through someone else?

Add to that, Jonathan was secure in who he was. In 1 Samuel 23:17, Jonathan tells David, "You will be king over Israel, and

I will be second to you" (NIV). He knew his role in God's plan. He made the decision to be a servant leader and help David thrive.

Do we have the humility to take a supporting role when that's what God calls us to do?

1 Samuel 18:4 says, "Jonathan took off the robe he was wearing and gave it to David, along with his tunic, and even his sword, his bow and his belt" (NIV). Jonathan didn't just offer words of support; he took concrete action to empower David.

How can you actively help someone else succeed?

Even when his father, King Saul, was trying to kill David, Jonathan remained loyal to his friend. He warned David of danger and encouraged him in the Lord.[35]

Our greatest legacy is not what we achieve ourselves, but whom we serve along the way.

Are you willing to stand by those you're called to serve, even when it's costly or unpopular?

Jonathan never became king. He never got what he technically "deserved." Yet, his impact thrived *through* David's reign.

---

[35] 1 Samuel 23:16–18.

Jonathan shows how our greatest legacy is not what we achieve ourselves, but whom we serve along the way.

Are you more concerned with your own success, or with the success of others and God's Kingdom?

God threads "Jonathan moments" throughout our days. He gives us opportunities to make the Influence Decision in a decidedly selfless way. Find ways to champion the dreams and callings of the people in your life. You'll quickly become an agent of encouragement, a lot like the next person we turn to—a guy who doesn't get much airtime, but has had an impact on each of our lives.

Service touches lives like few things can.

THE GREAT ENCOURAGER

Now let's turn to that encouraging figure, Barnabas in the New Testament. His name literally means "son of encouragement" and he lived up to it in every way.

First, like Jonathan, he saw potential in others.

When the newly-converted Paul (formerly Saul) tried to join the disciples in Jerusalem, they were all afraid of him. But Barnabas saw past Paul's history to his potential.

Do you have eyes to see the potential in others, even when it's not obvious?

Second, Barnabas was a bridge-builder.

Acts 9:27 tells us, "But Barnabas took him and brought him to the apostles..." (NIV) Barnabas used his influence to connect Paul with the apostles.

How can you use your relationships and influence to open doors for others?

Third, Barnabas invested in the growth of others.

In Acts 11:25–26, we see Barnabas seeking out Paul and bringing him to Antioch, where they ministered together for a year. Barnabas invested time and energy in Paul's development.

Are you willing to invest in others, even if it means sharing the spotlight?

Fourth, Barnabas was willing to forgive and offer a second chance.

In Acts 15:36–39, we see Barnabas standing up for John Mark, even when Paul didn't want to give him a second chance. Barnabas believed in restoration and growth.

Do you offer grace and second chances to those who have failed?

Fifth, Barnabas's acts of encouragement multiplied his impact.

By encouraging Paul and others, Barnabas multiplied his impact far beyond what he could have achieved alone. Paul went on to write almost 50 percent of the books in the New Testament and spread the gospel across the Roman world.

How can your encouragement today multiply your impact for God's Kingdom?

Sometimes, servant leadership means being the bridge that connects people to their God-given potential. Other times it means championing someone else's dreams. It could mean kneeling down to serve in ways that feel beneath you.

Each of these stories shows us what servant leadership looks like. There's not a better modern-day example of a servant leader than a man named Dick Hoyt. In 1977, a father and son started a journey that would inspire millions. Dick Hoyt, a thirty-six-year-old Air National Guard veteran, wasn't a runner. His son Rick, who was disabled and used a wheelchair, had a simple request: to run in a race together.

Their first five-mile run was challenging, but Rick's words after the race touched his father's heart: "Dad, when we were running, it felt like I was not disabled anymore."[36] This moment of joy and freedom sparked a lifelong mission.

---

[36] Rick Hoyt. "'When I'm Running, It Feels like I Am Not Disabled:' Lessons on Being a Great Teammate from the Best Team You've Never Heard Of." Changing the Game Project. Accessed October 30, 2024. https://changingthegameproject.com/im-running-feels-like-not-disabled-lessons-great-teammate-best-team-youve-never-heard/.

Team Hoyt in Wellesley. Photo courtesy of Wikimedia.

Determined to give his son more of these experiences, Dick began training daily. He pushed a wheelchair filled with a cement bag while Rick was at school, building his strength and endurance. His dedication paid off, and soon father and son were tackling bigger challenges together.

Over the years, Team Hoyt completed an astounding 1,130 endurance events. They ran marathons, competed in triathlons, and even crossed the entire United States in just forty-five days (which averages to eighty-three miles per day!). During swims, Dick pulled Rick in a boat. For biking, they used a special tandem bicycle. On runs, Dick pushed Rick's wheelchair with every stride.

Their perseverance and love touched hearts worldwide. A statue was erected in their honor, and they were inducted into the Ironman Hall of Fame. But more than any award, it was their bond and a lifetime of loving service that left a mark.

So, what makes a servant leader tick? What qualities set them apart? How do they think and act differently?

It's not about perfection, mind you. Even the greatest servant leaders, aside from Christ, have their flaws. But there are some core characteristics that show up again and again. Let's explore a few of them to help us make the Influence Decision.

HEART OF A SERVANT LEADER

A servant leader constantly looks for ways to add value to others.

As leadership expert Ken Blanchard said, "I think a great leader is somebody who realizes it's not about them, it's about the people that they're serving, that they're really other-directed rather than self-directed."[37]

This reminds me of the story of Millard Fuller, founder of Habitat for Humanity. In 1965, despite being a millionaire at twenty-nine, Fuller felt empty. He and his wife decided to give away their wealth and dedicate their lives to serving others. This led to founding Habitat for Humanity in 1976.

Fuller's vision was simple yet powerful: provide affordable housing to those in need by involving them in the building process. Under his leadership, Habitat has helped millions of people worldwide achieve homeownership. Isn't that amazing?

Fuller shows us first-hand how serving others creates lasting, transformative change. True fulfillment doesn't come from personal gain—but from wisely stewarding our resources to serve others.

You see, being "others-directed" isn't about low self-esteem or false modesty. It's about recognizing that your gifts, talents,

---

[37] Ken Blanchard. "Leadership Development Training & Consulting." BLANCHARD. Accessed October 30, 2024. https://www.blanchard.com/.

and abilities come from God, and they're meant to be used for something bigger than yourself—serving other people!

Paul referred to these qualities in 1 Thessalonians 2:7–8.

Gentleness: Strength under control

When you hear "gentle leader," what comes to mind? A pushover? Someone weak? That's not what we're talking about here. Biblical gentleness is strength under control.

Jesus described Himself as "gentle and humble in heart."[38] Yet, this is the same Jesus who drove money changers out of the Temple and stood up to corrupt religious leaders. His gentleness wasn't weakness; it was power channeled for the good of others.

Gentle leaders don't bully and coerce. They lead with care and compassion, but they're not afraid to be firm when necessary. They're like skilled surgeons—strong enough to cut where needed, but gentle enough to promote healing.

Generosity: Open hands, open heart

Servant leaders are generous—not just with their money, but with their time, energy, knowledge, and opportunities. They operate from an abundance mindset rather than a scarcity

---

[38] Matthew 11:29 (NIV).

mindset. They're always seeking to add value to others—even at their own expense.

Remember the little boy with five loaves and two fish? He gave what little he had, and Jesus multiplied it and used it to feed thousands. That's the kind of generosity we're talking about—a willingness to offer what we have, trusting God to multiply its impact.

Generosity isn't about how much you have; it's about what you do with what you have. A servant leader asks, "How can I use what I have to benefit others?"

Sacrificial Living: Daily choices, lasting impact

Here's where the rubber meets the road. Servant leadership isn't a one-time decision; it's a series of daily choices to put others before yourself. It's deciding to listen when you'd rather speak. It's staying late to help a colleague—even when you're tired. It's giving up your comfort for someone else's need, or serving on a volunteer team at your church—even when it's inconvient.

Paul puts it this way in Romans 12:1: "Therefore, I urge you, brothers and sisters, in view of God's mercy, to offer your bodies as a living sacrifice, holy and pleasing to God—this is your true and proper worship" (NIV).

Now, being a "living sacrifice" doesn't mean acting like a doormat or neglecting self-care. It means consistently choosing to use your life for the benefit of others and the glory of God.

SHINE THE LIGHT OF CHRIST

Jesus said, "You are the light of the world…" in Matthew 5:14. Servant leaders take this seriously. They understand their actions, attitudes, and words have the power to illuminate dark places and guide others toward truth and hope.

This isn't about drawing attention to yourself. It's about reflecting Christ's light in such a way that others are drawn to Him. It's about bringing clarity where there's confusion, hope where there's despair, and love where there's hatred.

In a world that often feels dark and cynical, servant leaders choose to shine. They refuse to be overcome by negativity, instead becoming beacons of positivity and possibility.

With this in mind, I want to challenge you. Look at these qualities—humility, gentleness, generosity, sacrificial living, and being a light. Which one resonates with you most? Which one challenges you?

Pick one. Just one. For the next week, focus on growing in that area. Look for opportunities to practice it in your daily life. You might be surprised at how this small shift can transform your leadership and influence.

It's one thing to talk about servant leadership; it's another to live it out. So let's get practical. How do we take these ideals and apply them in our day-to-day lives?

FINDING YOUR TOWEL MOMENT

Remember Jesus washing His disciples' feet? That was His "towel moment." It was a practical, humble act of service that spoke volumes. Your towel moment might look different, but the principle is the same.

Maybe you're a busy manager at work. Your towel moment could be making coffee for your team or staying late to help a new employee understand a project. Perhaps you're a stay-at-home parent. Your towel moment might be volunteering at your child's school or organizing a neighborhood cleanup.

The key is to look for practical ways to serve that might be "beneath" your perceived status. It's in those moments you have the opportunity to flip the script on what leadership looks like.

CHAMPIONING OTHERS' DREAMS

We talked about Jonathan earlier. He's a great example of championing someone else's dream, even when it cost him something. How can we do that in our everyday lives?

It could be as simple as genuinely celebrating a coworker's promotion, even if you were up for the same position. Or, maybe it's using your connections to help a young person get an internship in their field of interest.

Championing others isn't just about big gestures. It's about consistently looking for ways to help others succeed. It's about being genuinely happy when good things happen to those around you.

THE POWER OF ENCOURAGEMENT

Barnabas showed us the impact of consistent encouragement. In our world of cynicism and criticism, encouragement is revolutionary.

Start small. Make it a goal to genuinely encourage one person each day. It could be sending a text to a friend who's going through a tough time, writing a note of appreciation to a service worker, or publicly praising a team member's hard work.

Remember, encouragement isn't just about making people feel good. It's about giving others courage—the courage to keep going, to take risks, to become all God created them to be.

SERVING IN YOUR SPHERE OF INFLUENCE

You don't need a fancy title to be a servant leader. You just need to be intentional about serving where you are. Let's break it down by common spheres of influence.

1. **At home:** This is often the hardest place to be a servant leader. It's easy to take family for granted. But what if you decided

to be a servant at home? How would it change the way you interact with your spouse, kids, or roommates?

2. **At work:** Regardless of your position, you can be a servant leader at work. It might mean mentoring a younger colleague, being the first to volunteer for unpopular tasks, or simply being a positive presence in a stressful environment.

3. **In your community:** Look for needs in your neighborhood or town. Could you organize a meal train for a family going through a tough time? Volunteer at a local nonprofit? Coach a youth sports team?

4. **At church:** Your church likely has numerous opportunities to serve. Look for ways to truly lead through service, whether that's in children's ministry, greeting, or behind-the-scenes support.

THE DECISION THAT CHANGES EVERYTHING

We've journeyed through the heart of servant leadership, from Jesus washing feet to everyday heroes making a difference in their spheres of influence. Now it's time to make the Influence Decision for yourself.

Every time you decide to serve, to encourage, to put others first, you're growing as a servant leader and leading a thriving life. You're making a difference, whether you see it immediately or not.

A servant leader uses their God-given gifts, talents, and abilities to serve others and influence them for Christ.

As we wrap up, let's revisit our definition: a servant leader uses their God-given gifts, talents, and abilities to serve others and influence them for Christ. That's the heartbeat of the Influence Decision. It's about recognizing your gifts, your position, your relationships—they're all opportunities to serve and point others to Jesus.

Reflect

Take some time to process these questions, either in personal reflection or with others in your small group. Growth happens best in community, but honest individual reflection is essential for lasting change.

1. Last week's action step was to help someone grow in their relationship with God. How has that practice been for you throughout the week?

2. Which biblical example of servant leadership resonated with you most: Jesus, Jonathan, or Barnabas? Why?

3. What's one area of your life where you struggle to maintain a servant's heart? What makes it challenging?

4. Can you recall a time when someone's servant leadership made a significant impact on you? What did they do, and how did it affect you?

5. What's your "towel moment"? Is there an opportunity to serve that you've been hesitant to embrace?

6. How might your family, workplace, or community change if you consistently applied the principles of servant leadership?

Act

How can you add value to the people around you this week? Prayerfully think about your spheres of influence and jot down one idea for each line.

1. At work: _____

   _____

2. At church: _____

   _____

3. At home: _____

   _____

4. At school/in community: _____

   _____

Pray

Heavenly Father, thank You for the example of servant leadership we see in Jesus. Thank You for calling and equipping me to serve. Help me to see the opportunities around me to make a difference. Give me courage to serve even when it's uncomfortable or costly. May my life reflect Your love and draw others to You. Use me, Lord, to be an agent of change in my family, church, workplace, and community. In His name we pray. Amen.

CHAPTER 7

DECISION 6:
THE GENEROSITY DECISION

I CHOOSE TO LIVE GENEROUSLY

DID YOU KNOW generosity is contagious?

Researchers discovered this through a fascinating experiment. They gathered 240 strangers to play a simple game. Each person received twenty coins and had a choice: keep them all or share some with the group. The twist? Players were never to give to the same person twice.

You might expect people to be selfish. After all, why give away coins to strangers you'll never see again? But something surprising happened. When just one person chose to share, it sparked a chain reaction. Giving became contagious. The people they played with in the next round became more generous too. This effect didn't stop there. Those newly inspired players went on to influence others, who then inspired even more people.

This experiment shows us that even small acts of kindness can create a powerful ripple effect, touching lives far beyond our own. Like one domino falling after the next, a cascade of generosity started from just one gift. In this game, one person's kindness affected people up to three degrees of separation.

The scientists running the game, Dr. Fowler and Dr. Christakis, were shocked. They found that for every person who gave a coin away, three others were influenced to do the same. Much like a thriving garden, the generosity grew even as it spread.[39]

This wasn't just about coins. It showed how we affect each other without even knowing it—even with strangers we'd never see again.

Generosity is, in fact, contagious.

The science is in—generosity is, in fact, contagious. Now, if a game of coins with strangers in an experiment could start a chain reaction, just imagine what a God-inspired act of generosity could do.

In this chapter, I'm going to encourage you to make one of the most meaningful decisions of all—**The Generosity Decision**. A thriving life is built upon generosity in two directions: from

---

[39] Nicholas A. Christakis and James H. Fowler, "Cooperative Behavior Cascades in Human Social Networks," *Proceedings of the National Academy of Sciences of the United States of America* 107, no. 12 (2010): 5334–5338, https://doi.org/10.1073/pnas.0913149107.

God to us, and from us to each other. We are blessed to be a blessing on this earth. When we embrace generosity in our time, talents, and treasures, God meets us in life-changing ways.

THE AWE EFFECT

Have you ever stopped to really think about how generous God is? I mean, truly paused to consider the lavish abundance He's poured out all around us.

Let's talk about creation. God didn't have to make the world beautiful, but He did. He could have made everything plain, but instead, He painted the world with an impressive array of colors. From the bold hues of a sunset to the subtle shades of a flower petal, God's generosity is on full display in every color we see.

It doesn't stop there. Think about the sheer variety in nature. God didn't create just one type of tree or one kind of bird. No, He filled the earth with millions of species, each unique and remarkable in its own way.

All of this points to a God who delights in giving good gifts to His children. As James 1:17 says, "Every good gift and every perfect gift is from above, and comes down from the Father of lights, with whom there is no variation or shadow of turning."

Here's something truly incredible: God's generosity in creation doesn't just inspire us to stand in awe—it actually changes how we behave.

A fascinating study conducted by researchers at the University of California-Berkeley found that people who stood among towering eucalyptus trees for just one minute were more likely to help someone in need afterward.[40] They didn't even know they were part of an experiment. They were simply moved to help.

Imagine that—simply being in the presence of these majestic trees, creations of our generous God, made people more generous themselves. Here's the amazing thing—we're created in the image of this incredibly generous God. Generosity is woven into the very fabric of who we are. It's part of our DNA. Jesus is quoted in Acts 20:35 saying, "…It is more blessed to give than to receive" (NIV).

As believers, when we're generous, we're not just doing a nice thing. We're reflecting the character of our Creator. We're choosing to live out our true identity as children of our generous God.

Now, let's dive deeper into this incredible truth. If we want to experience tremendous freedom in our lives, we need to address a common myth. So many people think that their stuff belongs to them. Yet, the Bible teaches us something profoundly different.

The Scripture makes it clear that everything belongs to God. King David, a man after God's own heart, understood this deeply. In 1 Chronicles 29:11, he proclaims: "Yours, O LORD, is the greatness, the power and the glory, the victory and the

---

[40] Summer Allen, "The Science of Generosity," Greater Good Science Center, University of California-Berkeley, May 2018, https://ggsc.berkeley.edu/images/uploads/GGSC-JTF_White_Paper-Generosity-FINAL.pdf.

majesty; for all that is in heaven and in earth is Yours; Yours is the kingdom, O LORD, and You are exalted as head over all."

Take a moment to let that sink in. Say it out loud: "Yours!" It all belongs to God. Your life, your salvation, your family, your kids, your opportunities, your time, your business, your money—everything is His. And you know what? Realizing this is one of the most liberating experiences of your life.

Now, this doesn't mean we shrug off responsibility. Far from it! Instead, we're addressing the issue of ultimate ownership. God gives us these things for a reason. That's why the Bible introduces us to the principle of stewardship—an old English word that essentially means "manage it for someone else." God says, "It's My stuff, but I want you to look after it."

Your stuff is not your stuff.

Your stuff is not your stuff. Think of yourself as a manager. If you're managing something for someone else, you'd look after it with the owner's goals in mind. Right? That's exactly what God calls us to do. Here's the best part—when you steward His resources in a Christ-honoring way, He blesses you. One of the things my dad would tell me when I borrowed something from a neighbor was, "Whatever you do, bring it back better than you found it." That's stewardship!

In fact, I've come to see it all as a test. God is testing you with your influence, your business, your time, your money.

He's watching to see what you do with what He has entrusted to you. If you manage it well, He increases it even more.

As stewards, our generosity is tied to God's open hands.

As you'll see, it's not about how much you have to offer. It's about stewarding what you have so you can continue being generous to others.

God's generosity reaches its pinnacle in the person of Jesus Christ. John 3:16 tells us, "For God so loved the world that he gave his one and only Son, that whoever believes in him shall not perish but have eternal life" (NIV). God is the model for being a giver. He gave His very best for us.

> *Money is a wonderful tool but a lousy god.*

THREE DIMENSIONS OF GENEROSITY

When it comes to generosity, it's not just about what we give, but how we give our money. As disciples of Jesus, our giving should reflect the multifaceted nature of God's own generosity. Francis Bacon once wrote, "Money is a great servant but a bad master."[41] When we withhold the resources God's given to us, it indicates money has a hold on our hearts. Money is a wonderful tool but a lousy god.

---

[41] Francis Bacon, "Money is a great servant but a bad master," Goodreads, accessed October 10, 2024, https://www.goodreads.com/quotes/446478-money-is-a-great-servant-but-a-bad-master.

In Matthew 6:24, Jesus put it like this: "No one can serve two masters. Either you will hate the one and love the other, or you will be devoted to the one and despise the other. You cannot serve both God and money" (NIV). Generosity and giving are the ways to keep money in its proper place. We love God and use money, not the other way around.

Now, let's explore three key dimensions of giving: spontaneous, strategic, and sacrificial.

Dimension 1: Spontaneous Giving

I'll never forget a lesson my friend taught his children about spontaneous generosity. For years, every time they walked into a grocery store, he would turn to them and say, "Look around and pick out who you want to buy groceries for." Just like that, he transformed an ordinary shopping trip into an adventure in giving. They weren't wealthy—just committed to living generously.

Interestingly, science suggests that this kind of spontaneous generosity might be more natural to us than we think, especially when we're young. The study goes on to say toddlers exhibit more happiness when giving treats to others than when receiving treats themselves.[42]

This research hints at something profound. The impulse to give spontaneously and joyfully is part of being made in the

---

[42] Lara B. Aknin, J. Kiley Hamlin, and Elizabeth W. Dunn, "Giving Leads to Happiness in Young Children," *PloS one* 7, no. 6 (2012): e39211. doi:10.1371/journal.pone.0039211.

image of God. God has placed a seed of generosity in each of us, waiting to be nurtured and grown.

As adults, we're called to cultivate this attitude of spontaneous giving, to be alert to the needs around us and to be ready to respond at a moment's notice. It's about developing a generous spirit that's always on the lookout for opportunities to bless others, much like those naturally generous toddlers in the study.

> *God has placed a seed of generosity in each of us.*

In practice, this might look like:

- buying coffee for the person behind you in line

- leaving an extra-large tip for your server

- paying someone's car off as a surprise

Acts of spontaneous generosity, both small and large, make waves far beyond what we can see. By embracing spontaneous giving, we're not just doing good deeds—we're tapping into a fundamental aspect of being made in the image of God. We're deciding to live out the joyful, uninhibited generosity that is on full display as we reflect the heart of our generous Father.

How can you operate in spontaneous giving today or this week?

Dimension 2: Strategic Giving

While spontaneous giving is important, there's also a place for planned, purposeful generosity. This is about using our money in a deliberate way to make a lasting impact. Let's not forget the many positive ways money can help people.

Strategic giving involves things like:

- Practicing the biblical principle of tithing to your local church

- Financially supporting the poor, a missionary, a ministry, or a Project by giving an offering above your tithe

- Giving to holiday outreaches in your community

- Planned giving upon your death to your charities of choice

The Green family, who owns Hobby Lobby, has made a bold commitment to giving. David and Barbara Green are leading the charge, pledging to give away most of their wealth to support ministries around the world. As disciples of Jesus, they see their business success as a way to advance God's work on Earth—to the tune of billions in strategic giving.

Their ambitious and wide-reaching giving plan deeply inspires me. Every year, they donate over half of Hobby Lobby's pretax profits to ministries around the world.[43] This adds up to millions of dollars annually!

On this, David Green said, "We really wanted to do something that mattered a hundred years from now. Instead of just absorbing things ourselves, we wanted to do things in various ministries."

One of the standout projects they were the principal givers to is the $500 million Museum of the Bible in Washington DC, built to teach people about the Bible's history and impact. If you ever visit, remember the Generosity Decision built it.

In addition, they fund projects to translate the Bible into hundreds of languages. They even support archaeological digs in Israel related to biblical history. Their giving also reflects their values in many other ways.

The family takes a hands-on approach to their giving. To them, their wealth is a God-given responsibility, and they aim to be strategic in how they use it to further Christian causes.

---

[43] Fox Business. "Hobby Lobby Founder Explains Decision." Fox Business, accessed October 9, 2024, https://www. foxbusiness.com/retail/hobby-lobby-founder-explains-decision-give-away-ownership-company-joy-giving.

I love their family mission statement: "Love God Intimately, Live Extravagant Generosity." They're truly a family doing business for God.

Very few people are in a position to give away millions of dollars. Nevertheless, be strategic in your planned giving.

How can you strategically give this week, month, and year?

Dimension 3: Sacrificial Giving

The third dimension of giving is sacrificial—going beyond our comfort zone to meet the needs of others. This kind of giving costs us something significant, whether it's our time, our money, or our dreams.

The brilliant inventor and businessman R. G. LeTourneau gave sacrificially when he started practicing a "reverse tithe." This man of God chose radical generosity, living on 10 percent of his income and giving 90 percent away to mission work!

The following idea is often attributed to him: "It's not how much of my money I give to God, but how much of God's money I keep for myself."

That's the heart of sacrificial giving. The Bible says in 1 Chronicles 29:16, everything we have comes from God and belongs to Him.[44] LeTourneau experienced the joy of living open-handed time and again, crediting God for inspiring his amazing inventions.

His industry was literally earthmoving, building innovative ways for massive machines to push more dirt. His impact was earthmoving and *Heaven populating*, as he helped countless ministries to reach the world for Christ.

But sacrificial giving isn't just about large sums or grand gestures.

That reminds me of the story in the Bible of the widow's mite.[45] One day, Jesus watched as people placed their offerings into the temple treasury. Many wealthy individuals gave substantial amounts, making a show of their generosity. Then, a poor widow came forward and dropped in two small copper coins—all she had to live on. Jesus pointed out to His disciples that she had given more than anyone else. While others gave out of their abundance, she gave out of her poverty, sacrificing everything she had.

That's the essence of sacrificial giving. The widow's humble offering was small in monetary value, but immense in spiritual

---

[44] 1 Chronicles 29:16. "Lord our God, all this abundance that we have provided for building you a temple for your Holy Name comes from your hand, and all of it belongs to you" (NIV).

[45] Luke 21:1–4.

significance. She gave not from her surplus, but from her substance, demonstrating a profound trust in God to provide.

How can you operate in sacrificial giving?

"LIVE TO GIVE"

As disciples of Jesus, we're called to engage in all three dimensions of giving—spontaneous, strategic, and sacrificial. Each type of giving reflects a different aspect of God's character and allows us to participate in His work in unique ways. It's an exciting life.

"Live to give" was the motto of the famous missionary to Mexico, Wayne Myers.[46]

As we cultivate these dimensions of giving in our own lives, we'll find ourselves growing more and more into the character of our generous God. Therein lies another paradox of doing things God's way.

DO GOOD, FEEL GOOD

Generosity isn't just good for the receiver—it's incredibly beneficial for the giver too. I'm not just talking about warm, fuzzy feelings. Science backs this up with some fascinating discoveries.

---

[46] Myers, Wayne, and Mary Dunham Faulkner. *Living Beyond the Possible: Trusting God with Your Finances and Your Future.* (McLean, VA: Evangeline Press, 2003).

Neuroscientists have found that when we give, our brains activate the same reward system that lights up when we eat chocolate or receive gifts. It's like our brains are hardwired for generosity.

In the same study, researchers used MRI scans to look at people's brains while they made decisions about giving money to others. What they found was amazing. The areas of the brain associated with pleasure and social connection lit up when people chose to give. It's as if our brains are saying, "Yes! This is what you're meant to do!"[47]

STRESS LESS

But it's not just about brain activity. Generosity actually changes our body chemistry. When we give, our bodies release a blend of feel-good hormones:

- Serotonin, which helps regulate our mood

- Dopamine, which is associated with pleasure and motivation

- Oxytocin, often called the "love hormone," which promotes bonding and trust[48]

---

[47] Jorge Moll et al., "Human Fronto-Mesolimbic Networks Guide Decisions about Charitable Donation," *Proceedings of the National Academy of Sciences* 103, no. 42 (October 17, 2006): 15623–28, https://doi.org/10.1073/pnas.0604475103.

[48] William T. Harbaugh, et al., "Brain Imaging Reveals Joys of Giving," *Science* (2007), https://doi.org/10.1126/science.1157352.

At the same time, acts of generosity have been shown to reduce levels of cortisol, the stress hormone. So, not only does giving make us feel good, it actually helps combat stress. It's like a natural antidepressant and anti-anxiety medication rolled into one!

MENTAL AND EMOTIONAL GOOD

The benefits of generosity extend to our mental and emotional well-being too. Studies have shown that generous people report higher levels of happiness and life satisfaction. They tend to have a more positive outlook on life and a greater sense of purpose.

> *Happy people tend to be more generous, and generous acts make people happier.*

One researcher put it this way: "Generosity is both a cause and a consequence of happiness." In other words, happy people tend to be more generous, and generous acts make people happier. It's a beautiful, self-reinforcing cycle.[49]

---

[49] William T. Harbaugh et al., "Neural Responses to Taxation and Voluntary Giving Reveal Motives for Charitable Donations," *Science 316*, no. 5831 (2007): 1622–1625.

SOCIAL GOOD

Finally, let's not forget the social benefits of generosity. When we give, we strengthen our connections with others. We build trust, foster cooperation, and create a sense of community. Generous people tend to have stronger social networks and more satisfying relationships.

Remember that study about generosity being contagious? Well, it turns out not only are acts of generosity contagious, but the benefits of generosity are contagious too. When we give, we inspire others to give, sparking positivity and kindness in our communities.

Now, I want to be clear—we don't give in order to get these benefits. That would be missing the point entirely. We give because we're made in the image of a generous God, and because we want to bless others. But isn't it amazing that God has designed us in such a way that when we live as He intended, it's actually good for us too?

This reminds me of Proverbs 11:25, which says: "A generous person will prosper; whoever refreshes others will be refreshed" (NIV). Science is now confirming what Scripture has been telling us all along—generosity is a key to thriving!

So the next time you have an opportunity to be generous, remember, you're not just blessing someone else. You're also doing something profoundly good for yourself. You're activating your brain's reward system, releasing feel-good hormones, reducing stress, boosting your happiness, and strengthening your social connections. Making the Generosity Decision adds up to a healthier, happier, thriving life.

THE GENEROSITY HABIT

God wants to flood the world with generosity through His people. What would happen in our world if every disciple of Jesus developed a generosity habit? How could we impact hunger? Homelessness? Human trafficking? Poverty?

While none of us can make that happen on our own, we can change our decisions and play our part. We can work to make the Generosity Decision a habit—a reflex to help people in need. Generosity is like a muscle. The more you exercise it, the stronger it becomes.

As you practice these habits of generosity, you'll likely find they become more natural over time. You might even start to crave opportunities to give! That's the beautiful thing about generosity—the more we give, the more we want to give.

Remember, cultivating a generous spirit and attitude isn't about perfection. It's about progress. Just start, be consistent, and watch how God can use your generosity to bless others and transform your own life in the process.

In the words of Anne Frank, "No one has ever become poor by giving."[50] As you step out in generosity, you'll discover the profound truth of R. G. LeTourneau's words: "I shovel out the money, and God shovels it back—but God has a bigger shovel."[51]

MAKING THE GENEROSITY DECISION

As we wrap up our journey through the six decisions that will shape our lives, let's embrace this final decision: to live generously. This isn't just about what we do with our time, talents, and treasure. It's about who we choose to be at our core.

Remember, friends, the decision to live generously isn't just one more good thing to do. It's a fundamental shift in how we view God, ourselves, our

> *"No one has ever become poor by giving."*
> *—Anne Frank*

resources, and our purpose in this world. When we decide to live generously, we decide to live as God intended. We're deciding to thrive.

Go ahead and be generous, not because you have to, but because it's who you are as a child of God. As you do, you will

---

[50] Anne Frank. *The Diary of a Young Girl: The Definitive Edition*, ed. Otto H. Frank and Mirjam Pressler, trans. Susan Massotty. (New York: Doubleday, 1995).

[51] R.G. LeTourneau. *Mover of Men and Mountains: The Autobiography of R.G. LeTourneau.* (Chicago: Moody Publishers, 1967).

experience the fullness of life that comes from aligning your heart with the heart of our generous God.

Reflect

Take some time to process these questions, either in personal reflection or with others in your small group. Growth happens best in community, but honest individual reflection is essential for lasting change.

1. Last week's action step was to add value to those around you. How has that practice been for you throughout the week?

2. How have you seen generosity make a positive impact on your life or the lives of others?

3. What small act of spontaneous generosity can you practice this week?

4. In what ways can you be more strategic with your resources to bless others?

5. What is one area of your life where you feel God calling you to give sacrificially?

6. What fears or obstacles might be holding you back from living more generously?

7. How does reflecting on God's generosity toward you inspire you to live more generously?

Act

The decision is before us: Will we live with open hands or closed fists?

Living with closed fists means holding tightly to what we have, always fearing we won't have enough. It's a life of scarcity, where we look to our own hands to provide rather than God's.

Making the Generosity Decision leads to a life of abundance, recognizing that everything we have is a gift from God, meant to be shared. It's choosing to trust that our generous God will always provide what we need. It's experiencing the joy of being a conduit of God's blessings to others.

I want to challenge you to take one concrete step toward greater generosity this week. It doesn't have to be big. Perhaps it's finally making that donation you've been thinking about.

Whatever it is, take that step. As you do, pay attention to how it makes you feel. Notice the impact it has on others. I believe you'll start to experience firsthand the truth that it really is more blessed to give than to receive.

Pray

Heavenly Father, I thank You for Your incredible generosity toward me. You've given me life, salvation, and countless blessings. Help me to reflect Your generous nature in my life. Give me the courage to live with open hands, trusting in Your provision. Show me opportunities to be generous, and give me the wisdom and willingness to respond. May my life be marked by generosity, bringing glory to Your name and drawing others to You. In Jesus's name. Amen.

CHAPTER 8

DECIDE TO THRIVE

As we come to the end of our journey together, let's take a moment to reflect on the transformative power of the six decisions we've explored. These aren't just good ideas or helpful tips—they're life-altering decisions. They're the keys to unlocking the thriving life God designed for you.

Remember, you were designed to thrive–not just to survive. You can flourish in every area of your life. God wants you to experience life in all its fullness, and these six decisions are the pathways to that life.

Let's revisit each decision and consider how they work together to create a thriving life.

1. The Priority Decision: I choose to put God first every day.

This is the foundation of everything else. When we decide to put God first, we're aligning our lives with the very purpose for which we were created. We're acknowledging that He is the source of all life, wisdom, and goodness. This decision changes everything—how we see the world, how we spend our time, how we make decisions.

Putting God first doesn't mean neglecting other important areas of life. Rather, it means filtering everything through the lens of our relationship with Him. It means starting each day by connecting with God, seeking His guidance, and surrendering our plans to His will.

When we make this decision consistently, we begin to see life from God's perspective. Our priorities shift. Our values align more closely with His. We find a sense of peace and purpose that can't be shaken by circumstances.

2. The Relationship Decision: I choose to pursue life-giving relationships.

We were created for connection—with God and others. This decision recognizes the vital importance of healthy relationships in our lives. It's about intentionally cultivating relationships that encourage and support us in our journey of faith.

You become like the people you spend the most time with. By choosing to surround yourself with people who are also pursuing God and personal growth, you're creating an environment that nurtures your own growth.

This decision also involves willingness to be vulnerable and to open yourself to others. It means being intentional about building deep, meaningful connections rather than settling for surface-level acquaintances.

As you make this decision daily, you'll find yourself part of a community that reflects God's love and grace. You'll have people to celebrate with in times of joy and to lean on in times of struggle.

3. The Purpose Decision: I choose to reach people for Christ.

This decision aligns your life with God's mission in the world. It's about recognizing that you're not just saved from something, but saved for something. God has uniquely positioned you to reach people that no one else can reach.

Making this decision means living with intentionality. It means seeing every interaction as an opportunity to show God's love and share His message. It's not about being pushy but about living in such a way that others are drawn to the hope and joy they see in you.

As you consistently make this decision, you'll find a deep sense of purpose and fulfillment. You'll see how God can use your story and your experiences—even your struggles—to impact others for eternity.

4. The Growth Decision: I choose to grow daily and help others do the same.

Growth doesn't happen by accident. It requires intentional effort and consistent choices. This decision is about committing to lifelong learning and development—not just for your own sake, but for others as well.

Making this decision means being willing to step out of your comfort zone. It means embracing challenges as opportunities for growth. It involves being honest about your weaknesses and actively working to overcome them.

As you make this decision day after day, you'll find yourself becoming more like Christ as you grow as His disciple. You'll develop new skills, gain wisdom, and increase your capacity to impact others. As you help others grow, you'll find that you grow even more.

5. The Influence Decision: I choose to make a difference through my unique gifts, talents, and abilities.

God has given you a unique set of gifts, talents, and abilities. This decision is about stewarding those gifts well and using them to make a positive impact in the world.

Making this decision means rejecting the lie that you have nothing to offer. It means stepping out in faith to use your gifts, even when you feel inadequate. It's about recognizing that your influence—no matter how small it may seem—can have a ripple effect that extends far beyond what you can see.

As you consistently make this decision, you'll discover new ways to serve and contribute to others. You'll find fulfillment in using your gifts for a purpose greater than yourself.

6. The Generosity Decision: I choose to live generously.

This final decision is perhaps the most countercultural of all. In a world that often encourages us to hoard and protect what we have, choosing to live generously is a radical act. It's a decision that reflects the heart of our generous God.

Making this decision means living with open hands, recognizing that everything we have is a gift from God. It's about being willing to share not just our money, but our time, our talents, our homes, our very lives.

As you consistently choose generosity, you'll experience the paradoxical truth that giving leads to greater joy and fulfillment than receiving. You'll become a conduit of God's blessings to others, and in the process, you'll find yourself blessed beyond measure.

HOW TO KEEP THRIVING

These six decisions work together in symphony, each one reinforcing and amplifying the others. As you put God first, you'll be better equipped to build healthy relationships. As you pursue God's purpose, you're motivated to grow. As you use your influence, you have more opportunities to be generous. It's a beautiful, self-reinforcing cycle of thriving.

Now, I want to be clear—making these decisions doesn't guarantee a problem-free life. You'll still face challenges, setbacks, and difficult seasons. But these decisions provide a framework and foundation for navigating life's ups and downs with purpose, resilience, and joy.

So, what now? How do you move forward from here?

Recognize that change doesn't happen overnight.

It's the result of small, consistent decisions made day after day. Don't try to overhaul your entire life at once. Instead, choose one or two areas to focus on. Which of these six decisions resonates most with you right now? Where do you see the greatest need or opportunity for growth in your life?

Once you've identified your focus areas, set specific and achievable goals. Make it something concrete you can act on daily. For example, if you're focusing on the Priority Decision, your goal might be to spend the first fifteen minutes of each day in prayer and Bible reading. If it's the Relationship Decision, you might commit to reaching out to one person each day with encouragement.

Build accountability.

Share your goal with a trusted friend, family member, or mentor. Ask them to check in with you regularly and encourage you in your journey. Consider joining a small group or finding a spiritual growth partner who can walk alongside you.

Remember you're not on this journey alone.

As a believer, you have the Holy Spirit within you, empowering you to make these decisions and live them out. You're part of a community of believers who are also living for God. Lean on these resources. Draw strength from God's presence and the support of your community.

Be prepared for resistance.

Old habits and patterns will try to reassert themselves. You may face discouragement or setbacks. In those moments, remind yourself of why you started this journey. Don't forget you also have an adversary that will attempt to resist you at every turn. James 4:7 says, "Therefore submit to God. Resist the devil and he will flee from you." Remember that you were created to thrive, and that God is working in you, shaping you into the person He created you to be.

Be on the lookout for God's work in your life.

As you make these decisions, you'll likely start to notice changes—maybe subtle at first but growing over time. You will find yourself more at peace, more joyful, more confident in your purpose. You will see your relationships deepening or new opportunities for influence opening up. Celebrate these changes, giving thanks to God for His transformative work in your life.

Finally, be patient with yourself.

Growth is a process. There will be days when you feel like you're making great progress, and days when you feel like you're taking two steps back. That's normal. The key is to keep making the decision to move forward, one day at a time.

As we close, I want to leave you with a powerful truth from Scripture. In Philippians 1:6, the apostle Paul writes: "Being confident of this, that he who began a good work in you will carry it on to completion until the day of Christ Jesus" (NIV). God isn't finished with you yet. He's continuing to work in your life, and He will be faithful to complete the good work He's started.

These six decisions shape you into the person He created you to be. As you consistently choose to put God first, pursue healthy relationships, live out your purpose, commit to growth, use your influence, and live generously, you're cooperating with God's work in your life.

So, step out in faith. Decide to thrive. Choose, day by day, to align your life with God's Word, Will, and Way—and watch in awe as He works in and through you in ways you never imagined possible.

May your journey of growth and transformation be blessed. May you experience the fullness of life that God intends for you. May your life be a testament to the transformative power of Christ and the daily decisions that build a life that consistently thrives.

Remember, six daily decisions, rooted in six biblical values, result in a thriving life!

ABOUT THE AUTHOR

Steve Robinson is a speaker, author, and founding pastor of Church of the King—which reaches thousands across six physical locations, an online campus with members worldwide, and daily television and radio broadcasts. His books include *Perspective Shift*, *Extraordinary Living*, *Simple Prayer*, and *Hope Again*.

Pastor Steve grew up in New Orleans and is a graduate of Tulane University. He holds a Doctor of Ministry degree from Southeastern University in Lakeland, Florida. His experiences leading Church of the King through the regional devastation of Hurricane Katrina and the global turmoil of the Great Recession inspired his doctoral thesis, which focuses on trauma, leadership, and healing.

Pastor Steve serves on the boards of Equip, a worldwide leadership organization led by John Maxwell, and Oral Roberts University in Tulsa, Oklahoma. His passion is to see people who are far from God reached and discipled into fully devoted followers of Christ. He and his wife, Jennifer, live in a suburb of New Orleans, Louisiana, and are blessed with four children and one son-in-law: Isabelle and her husband Stone, Conrad, William, and Annaliese.